BRUCE LEE'S
FIGHTING METHOD
THE COMPLETE EDITION

Bruce Lee and M. Uyehara

BRUCE LEE'S
FIGHTING METHOD
THE COMPLETE EDITION

Bruce Lee and M. Uyehara

Edited by Sarah Dzida, Jon Sattler and Jeannine Santiago

Art Design by John Bodine

Project Supervision by Raymond Horwitz

Library of Congress Control Number: 2008933954
ISBN-10: 0-89750-170-5
ISBN-13: 978-0-89750-170-5

Third Printing 2011

WARNING

BLACK BELT BOOKS
A Division of **OHARA** **PUBLICATIONS, INC.**
World Leader in Martial Arts Publications

Foreword

Bruce Lee's original idea for *Fighting Method* was to write an exclusive, limited edition book (not more than 200 copies) on *jeet kune do*. He had the pictures taken for this purpose. The photos were taken in late 1967 after my father had coined the term "jeet kune do." However, after the pictures were done, he changed his mind about publishing a JKD book. Later in 1972 and 1973, my father began to work again on sequencing these same photos and writing captions for them, so it is possible that he was reconsidering the project at that time.

For his book, Bruce Lee wanted the action to be as realistic as possible, which is why he sought out photographers who could help depict the action in real time. For many of the shots, he used a high-speed camera to capture the movements. The photos taken at Bruce's school were all shot in two days. Other shots were taken in front of Bruce's house, in his backyard, and outside *Black Belt*'s offices.

To ensure the action was realistic, my father also insisted that the strikes make real contact. He did not use full power when making contact because he didn't want to injure anyone, but he was adamant that the action look as real as possible. Ted Wong recalls that when he had to take a kick from Bruce Lee, he wore a kendo chest protector, but Bruce was concerned that this would not be enough. So Ted tore up cardboard boxes and stuffed the pieces into his clothing to help protect his body from the impact. And even though Ted was black and blue at the end of the day, the shoot still remains a very fond memory of his.

Without the help of Dan Inosanto, Ted Wong, Joe Bodner, Oliver Pang, Mito Uyehara, Linda Lee, and, of course, Bruce Lee, this book on Bruce Lee's fighting method would never have come into being. Many thanks to *Black Belt*, Rainbow Publications, Ohara Publications and Active Interest Media for their help and continued support of Bruce Lee's books and legacy. A special thank you to Ted Wong for his help in updating the books. We hope you enjoy this new and complete edition of *Bruce Lee's Fighting Method*.

—Shannon Lee
2008

Introduction

This book was in the making in 1966 and most of the photographs were shot in 1967. The late Bruce Lee intended to publish this book years ago but decided against it when he learned that martial arts instructors were using his name to promote themselves. It was quite common to hear comments like "I taught Bruce Lee" or "Bruce Lee taught me jeet kune do." And Bruce may never have seen or known these martial artists.

Bruce didn't want people to use his name to promote themselves or their schools with false pretenses. He didn't want them to attract students this way, especially the young teens.

But after his death, his widow, Linda, felt that Bruce had contributed so much in the world of the martial arts that it would be a great loss if the knowledge of Bruce would die with him. Although the book can never replace the actual teaching and knowledge that Bruce Lee possessed, it will enhance you, the serious martial artist, in developing your skill in fighting.

Bruce always believed that all martial artists train diligently for one single purpose—to defend themselves. Whether we are in judo, karate, aikido, kung fu, etc., our ultimate goal is to prepare ourselves for any situation.

To train yourself for this goal, you must train seriously. Nothing is taken for granted. "You have to kick or punch the bag with concentrated efforts," Bruce used to say. "If you are going to train without the concept that this is the real thing, you are shortchanging yourself. When you kick or punch the bag, you have to imagine that you are actually hitting an adversary. Really concentrating, putting 100 percent in your kicks and punches, is the only way you are going to be good."

If you have not read *Tao of Jeet Kune Do* by Bruce Lee, please read it. It was meant to complement this book, and the knowledge from both books will give you a full picture of Brucc's art.

—M. Uyehara

Contents

PART I BASIC TRAINING

Chapter 1 **The Fighting Man's Exercise** _____ **7**
Aerobic Exercises
Warming-Up Exercises
Flexibility Exercises
Abdominal Exercises

Chapter 2 **The On-Guard Position** _____ **21**
Stances
Balance

Chapter 3 **Footwork** _____ **41**
The Shuffle
Quick Movements
Quick Retreat
The Burst
Side Stepping

Chapter 4 **Power Training** _____ **59**
Punching Power
Pulling Power
Power Kicking

Chapter 5 **Speed Training** _____ **87**
Speed in Punching
Nontelegraphic Punch
Speed in Kicking
Awareness

PART II SKILL IN TECHNIQUES

Chapter 6 **Skill in Movement** _____ **119**
Distance
Footwork
Side Stepping and Ducking

Chapter 7 **Skill in Hand Techniques** _____ **137**
JKD vs. Classical
Punching Straight
Bad Habits
Trapping and Grabbing

Chapter 8 **Skill in Kicking** _____ **165**
Leading Side Kick to High Kick
Hook Kick
Spin Kick
Other Kicks

Chapter 9 **Parrying** _____ **183**
Inside High Parry
Inside Low Parry
Outside High Parry
JKD vs. Classical
Parrying vs. Blocking

Chapter 10 **Targets** _____ **207**
Primary Targets
Vital Spots
Correct Use of Arsenals

Chapter 11 **Sparring** _____ **219**
Stance
Feinting and Drawing
Body Motion
Bad Habits

PART III ADVANCED TECHNIQUES

Chapter 12   **Hand Techniques for Offense** *(Part A)* _____ **237**
Leading Finger Jab
Leading Straight Right
Lead to Body
Straight Left

Chapter 13   **Hand Techniques for Offense** *(Part B)* _____ **265**
Straight Left to the Body
Lead Jab
Backfist
Hook Punch
Uppercut

Chapter 14   **Attacks With Kicks** _____ **287**
Leading Shin and Knee Kick
Leading Side Kick
Hook Kick
Spin Kick
Sweep Kick

Chapter 15   **Defense and Counter** _____ **313**
Leading Finger Jab
Leading Right
Shin or Knee Kick
Side Stop-Kick
Hook Kick
Spin Kick

Chapter 16   **Five Ways of Attack** *(by Ted Wong)* _____ **339**
Simple Angle Attack
Hand-Immobilizing Attack
Progressive Indirect Attack
Attack by Combination
Attack by Drawing

Chapter 17   **Attributes and Tactics** _____ **351**
Speed
Timing
Attitude
Tactics

PART IV SELF-DEFENSE TECHNIQUES

Chapter 18   **Defense Against a Surprise Attack** _____ **365**

Chapter 19   **Defense Against an Unarmed Assailant** _____ **375**

Chapter 20   **Defense Against Grabbing** _____ **389**

Chapter 21   **Defense Against Choke Holds and Hugs** _____ **411**

Chapter 22   **Defense Against an Armed Assailant** _____ **425**

Chapter 23   **Defense Against Multiple Assailants** _____ **451**

Chapter 24   **Defense From a Vulnerable Position** _____ **469**

Index _____ **478**

PART I
BASIC TRAINING

Chapter 1
The Fighting Man's Exercise

The Fighting Man's Exercise

Aerobic Exercises

One of the most neglected elements of martial artists is the physical workout. Too much time is spent on developing skill in techniques and not enough in physical participation.

Practicing your skill in fighting is important, but so is maintaining your overall physical condition. Actually both are needed to be successful in a real fight. Training is a skill of disciplining your mind, developing your power and supplying endurance to your body. Proper training is for the purpose of building your body and avoiding activities or substances that will deteriorate or injure it.

Bruce Lee was a specimen of health. He trained every day and consumed only the proper food. Although he drank tea, he never drank coffee—instead he normally consumed milk. He was a martinet who never let his work interfere with his training. Even when he was sent to India to find suitable locations for filming, he took along his running shoes.

Lee's daily training consisted of aerobic exercises plus others, which were patterned to develop his skill in fighting. He varied his exercises to avoid boredom. One of his favorite exercises was running four miles a day in 24 to 25 minutes. He would change his tempo while running—after several miles of constant, even strides, he would sprint several feet and then return to easier running. Between changes in running tempo, he would also shuffle his feet. Lee was not particular where he ran: at the beach, in parks or woods, up and down hills or on surfaced streets, as in photo 1.

Besides running, he also rode an Exercycle to develop his endurance, legs and cardiovascular muscles, as in photo 2. He usually rode at full speed—35 to 40 miles per hour continuously for 45 minutes to an hour. Frequently, he would ride his Exercycle right after his running.

Another aerobic exercise that Lee scheduled in his routine was skipping rope, which you can adopt. This exercise not only develops your stamina and leg muscles but also improves your agility, making you "light on your feet." Only recently, physiologists have learned, by several tests, that skipping rope is more beneficial than jogging. Ten minutes of skipping rope is equivalent to 30 minutes of jogging. Both are very beneficial exercises for the cardiovascular system.

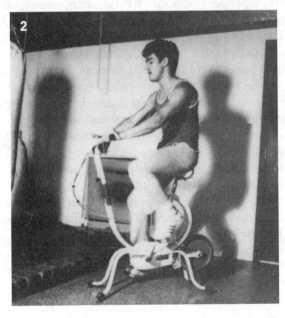

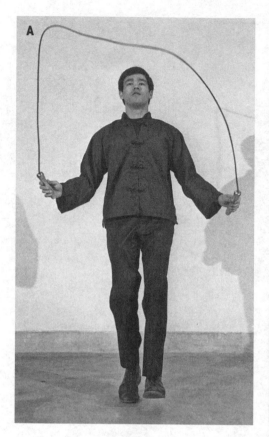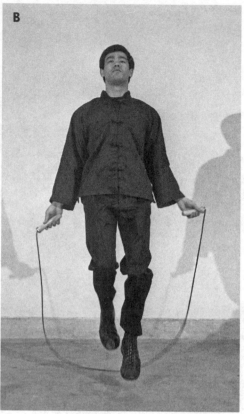

Skipping rope properly is one of the best exercises for developing a sense of balance. First, skip on one foot, as in photo A, holding the other in front of you, then rotate your foot, as in photo B, skipping on the alternate foot with each revolution of the rope, from a gradual pace to a really fast tempo. Minimize your arm-swing; instead, use your wrists to swing the rope over. Lift your foot slightly above the ground, just enough for the rope to pass. Skip for three minutes (equivalent to a round in a boxing match), then rest one minute only before you continue for another round. Three rounds of this exercise are sufficient for a good workout. As you become conditioned to skipping, you can omit the rest period and do the exercise for as long as 30 minutes straight. The best rope is made of leather with ball bearings in the handles.

Additional endurance exercises are shadowboxing and actual sparring. Shadowboxing is a good agility exercise that also builds up your speed. Relax your body and learn to move easily and smoothly. At first, concentrate on your form, as in photo C and move with lightness on your feet until it becomes natural and comfortable—then work faster and harder. It is a good idea to start your workout with shadowboxing to loosen your muscles. Imagine that your worst enemy stands before you and that you are going to demolish him. If you use your imagination intensely, you can instill into yourself an almost real fighting frame of mind. Besides developing stamina, shadowboxing increases your speed, creates ideas and establishes techniques to be used spontaneously and intuitively. Going several rounds is the best way to learn proper footwork.

Too many beginners are too lazy to drive themselves. Only by hard and continuous exercise will you develop endurance. You have to drive yourself to the point of exhaustion ("out of breath") and expect muscle ache in a day or two. The best endurance training method seems to be a lengthy period of exercise interspersed with many brief but high-intensity endeavors. Aerobic, stamina-type exercises should be done gradually and cautiously increased. Six weeks of this kind of training is a minimum for any sport that requires considerable amounts of endurance. It takes years to be in peak condition and, unfortunately, stamina is quickly lost when you cease to maintain high conditioning exercises. According to some medical experts, you lose most of your benefit from exercises if you skip more than a day between workouts.

Warming-Up Exercises

To warm up, select light, easy exercises to loosen your muscles and prepare them for more strenuous work. Besides improving your performance, warm-up exercises are necessary to prevent injury to your muscles. No smart athlete will use his hands or legs violently without first warming them up carefully. These light exercises should dictate as closely as possible the ensuing, more strenuous types of movements.

How long should you warm up? This depends on several aspects. If you live in a colder area, or train during the cold winter, you have to do longer warm-up exercises than those who live in a warmer climate. Longer warm-ups are recommended in the early morning than in the afternoon. Generally, five or ten minutes of warm-up exercises are adequate, but some performers need much more. A ballet dancer spends at least two hours warming up. He commences with very basic movements, gradually but consistently increasing the activity and intensity until he is ready to make his appearance.

Flexibility Exercises

Bruce Lee learned that certain exercises can help you greatly in your performance, and others can impede or even impair your execution of techniques. He found that beneficial exercises are those that do not cause antagonistic tension in your muscles.

Your muscles respond differently to different exercises. During a static or slow exercise such as a handstand or lifting heavy weights such as a barbell, the muscles on both sides of the joints operate strongly to set the body in a desirable position. But in a rapid activity such as running, jumping or throwing, the muscles that close the joints contract and the muscles directly opposite elongate to allow the movement. Although there is still tension on both muscles, the strain is considerably less on the elongated, or lengthened one.

When there is excessive or antagonistic tension on the elongated muscles, it hinders and weakens your movement. It acts like a brake, causing premature fatigue, generally associated only with a new activity that demands different muscles to perform. A coordinated, natural athlete is able to perform in any sporting activity with ease because he moves with little antagonistic tension. On the other hand, the novice performs with excessive tension and effort, creating a lot of wasted motions. Although this coordination trait is a more natural talent in some than in others, all can improve it by intensive training.

Here are some of the exercises that you can adapt to your daily training. For flexibility, place your foot on a railing or object, as in photos A and B, keeping your leg horizontal to the ground—it could be slightly lower or higher, depending on your flexibility.

For the beginner, do not attempt any strenuous exercise. Instead, after placing your foot on the railing, just move your toes toward you, keeping your extended foot flexed straight, as in photo A. After a few minutes, rotate your foot. In a few days, as your leg muscles are limbered, you can proceed to the next step, as in photo B. Press your knee to keep your leg straight and lean forward from the hip as much as possible without injuring your

muscles. From this exercise, you then proceed to emulate photo C. Keeping your extended leg straight, push your hand downward. As you progress, you'll notice that you are also beginning to lean forward, putting more stress on your leg muscles. Finally, you are able to touch your toes, as in photo D. After some months, you may be able to wrap your hand around your foot, as in photo E, even with the support raised higher.

Other leg-flexibility exercises include leg splits and hanging leg raises, as in photo F. To do this exercise, use a long rope supported by a pulley. A noose encircles your foot. Pull the other end of the rope to the maximum height that your leg muscles will bear without hurting yourself. Try to keep your foot horizontally aligned throughout the exercise. This exercise allows you to execute high side kicks. You should rotate your legs in all these exercises.

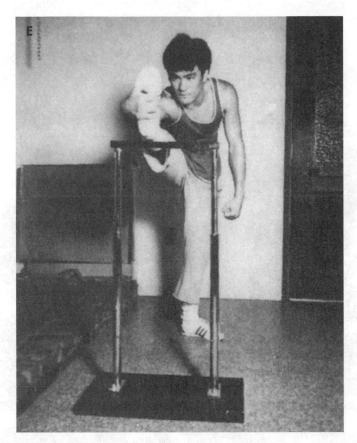

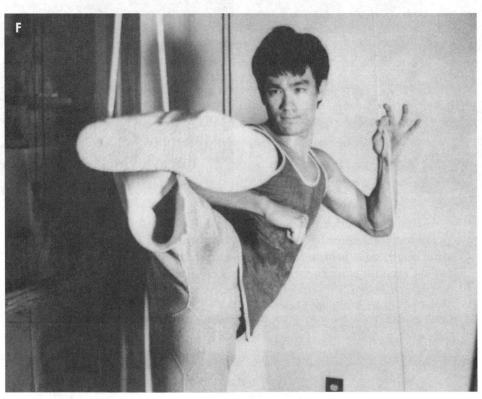

Advanced students who like to do exceptionally high kicks can progress to trampoline exercises. In photo G, Lee uses two light dumbbells and jumps high to develop both balance and springy legs. Once he can control his body on a trampoline, he attempts leg splits, as in photo H; a high front kick, as in photo I; and a flying side kick, as in photo J.

Other limbering exercises include body stretches. After you have developed elasticity in your leg muscles, you should be able to stretch your body as far back as possible, then bend forward as far as possible, until your head is touching your knees, as in photos K, L and M.

Abdominal Exercises

No one could help but notice Lee's abdominal muscles. "One of the most important phases of fighting," he used to say, "is sparring. In order to spar, you must be able to take punches in your midsection." To do this, Lee concentrated on several exercises that you can also adopt. The most popular are the sit-ups on a slant board, as in photo N (see page 18). Secure your feet, bend your knees and, after placing your hands behind your head, lift your body toward your feet. Do as many as you can until you feel the strain around your abdomen. After reaching 50 to 100 repetitions, you can place a weight such as a dumbbell or barbell plate behind your neck and do your sit-ups.

Another excellent way of doing sit-ups is to sit at the edge of a bench, have someone secure your ankles and lower your body as far down as possible toward the floor. This exercise stretches your midsection much more, but it is more difficult to do. If you have a chinning bar (pull-up bar), you can also develop your abdominal muscles by hanging onto the bar with both hands and slowly lifting both legs until they are extended horizontally. Keep them in that position for as long as possible and try to beat your last record each time you do the exercise. Buy one of those kitchen timers to help you keep track of the time.

Another excellent exercise is the leg raise. Lie on the floor, keeping your back flat on it by pushing in your midsection and lifting your head slightly until you can see your feet. Keep your legs together and straight. Then lift them upward slowly and as high as possible. Then slowly return them to the floor.

To get the most out of this exercise, do not let your feet touch the floor—keep them about an inch above the floor and start to raise them again. Do as many repetitions as possible. If you have a weight-lifting bench, you can do the same exercise, as in photo O. This exercise is also good for your lower back muscles.

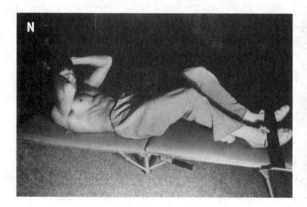
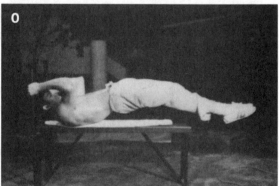

One advantage in doing an abdominal exercise is that it can be done while you are doing other activities. For instance, Lee used to watch television while lying on the floor with his head slightly up and keeping his feet spread out and slightly above the floor.

To toughen your midsection, get a medicine ball and have someone drop it on your abdomen, as in photos P and Q. To vary your exercise, you can also have someone throw it directly to your midsection. Let the ball hit your body before catching it. See photos R and S.

If you do your workout alone, you can use your heavy punching bag as a substitute for the medicine ball. Swing the heavy bag and let it hit your body. You can adjust the spot of impact either by moving forward or backward. If you want a heavier impact, swing the bag harder.

In your daily life, there's always an opportunity for more supplemental exercises. For instance, park your car several blocks from your destination and walk briskly. Avoid the elevator and use the stairs instead. While climbing the stairs, you can have a good workout either by running up or by skipping a step or two.

Chapter 2
The On-Guard Position

FRONT VIEW

SIDE VIEW

The On-Guard Position

Stances

The most effective jeet kune do stance for attacking and defending is the on-guard position. This semi-crouch stance is perfect for fighting because your body is sturdy at all times and in a comfortably balanced position to attack, counter or defend without any forewarning movements. It provides your body with complete ease and relaxation but, at the same time, allows quick reaction time. From this stance, the movement is not jerky but smooth and prepares your next move without any restriction. It creates an illusion or "poker body" to your opponent—concealing your intended movements.

The on-guard position is perfect for mobility. It allows you to take small steps for speed and controlled balance while bridging the distance to your opponent, and it camouflages your timing. Because the leading hand and foot are closest to the target, 80 percent of the hitting is done by them. Bruce Lee, a natural right-hander, adopted the "southpaw" or "unorthodox" stance because he believed that the stronger hand and foot should do most of the work.

BACK VIEW

INCORRECT

It is important to position your arms, feet and head correctly. From the southpaw stance, the chin and shoulder should meet halfway—the right shoulder raised an inch or two and the chin dropped about the same distance. At this position, the muscles and bone structure are in the best possible alignment, protecting the point of the chin. In close-in fighting, the head is held vertically with the edge of the chin pressed to the collarbone and one side of the chin tucked to the lead shoulder. Only in rare, extreme defensive maneuvers would the point of the chin be tucked into the lead shoulder. This would angle your head and turn your neck into an unnatural position. Fighting in this position would tense the lead shoulder and arm, prevent free action and cause fatigue because you would lack support of the muscles and straight bone alignment.

The leading hand position could be placed slightly below shoulder height, as in photos A and A1 (close-up shot). In photos B and B1, pay close attention to the extension of both Lee's right and left hand. Photos C and C1 reveal another view of his stance from the back, showing his leading hand more clearly.

In photo Y, both fighters stand in the on-guard position incorrectly. The person on the left has his right foot too wide

RIGHT LEAD STANCE
(southpaw)

Head: Avoid blows by bobbing and weaving.

Right Shoulder: Slightly raised and chin slightly lowered to protect your chin and part of your face on the lower right side.

Right Hand: Heavily depended on for striking. It protects your face and your groin.

Right Elbow: Defends the midsection and the right side of your body.

Right Knee: Slightly turned inward to defend the groin area.

Right Foot: At a 25- to 30-degree angle and depended on heavily for kicking.

Left Hand: Heavily depended on for defense. It protects your face plus your groin.

Left Forearm: Defends the midsection of your body.

Left Elbow: Defends the left side of your body.

Left Foot: At a 45- to 50-degree angle and the heel is raised for greater mobility. It has to be ready to trigger your body forward like a coiled spring.

and reveals too much of his body. The person on the right has his right foot too far to his left, restricting his movement and keeping him off-balance.

Sometimes, but very seldom, you can adopt the low-line position without a lead because many fighters are not prepared for such a defense. This type of position may confuse your opponent and severely hamper and, to a certain extent, check his offensive assault. Your exposed head is now a target but can be protected by mobility and relying on being a safe distance away from him.

The rear hand is held four to five inches from your body in the on-guard position with the elbow protecting the lower

LEFT LEAD STANCE
(orthodox)

Head: Avoid blows by bobbing and weaving.

Left Shoulder: Slightly raised and chin slightly lowered to protect your chin and part of your face on the lower left side.

Right Hand: Heavily depended on for defense. It protects your face plus your groin.

Left Hand: Heavily depended on for striking. It protects your face and your groin.

Right Forearm: Defends the midsection of your body.

Left Elbow: Defends the midsection and the left side of your body.

Right Elbow: Defends the right side of your body.

Left Knee: Slightly turned inward to defend the groin area.

Right Foot: At a 45- to 50-degree angle and the heel is raised for greater mobility. It has to be ready to trigger your body forward like a coiled spring.

Left Foot: At a 25- to 30-degree angle and depended on heavily for kicking.

ribs and the forearm gently brushing your body, defending the midsection. The rear hand is aligned with the lead shoulder and placed almost to the chest of that shoulder.

The lead foot dictates the position of the trunk. If the lead foot is properly in place, then the trunk automatically assumes the correct position. It is important that the trunk form a straight line with the lead leg. As the lead foot is turned inward, the body consequently moves in the same direction, displaying a narrow target to the opponent. If, however, the lead foot is turned outward, the body is squared, presenting a larger target. For defense, the narrow target obviously is more advantageous, but the square blends in better for launching some attacks.

A

Good form is essential to your stance. It allows you to perform in the most efficient manner with a minimum of lost movement and wasted energy. Eliminate the nonessential motions and muscle activity, which causes exhaustion without gaining any benefit. Both of your arms and shoulders must be relaxed and loose, to whip out and snap your fists like thrusts from a rapier. Keep your lead hand or both hands in constant "weaving" motion, but always keep yourself covered while doing it. The lead hand should be constantly moving, flickering in and out like a snake's tongue ready to strike. This threatening motion keeps your opponent in a bewildering plight.

Remember, if you tense up, you lose your balance, timing and flexibility, which are essential to all proficient fighters. Although relaxation is a physical form, it is controlled by your mind. You have to learn, by conscious effort, to direct your thoughts and body into this new habit of muscular activity. Relaxation is a state of muscular tension. It is natural to have a slight degree of tension in your muscles when performing any physical activity. But your antagonistic muscles must retain a low degree of tension to perform coordinated, graceful and efficient movements. Through constant practice, you can achieve this feeling of relaxation at will. Once you have acquired this, you should induce this attitude in a potentially tension-created environment.

Use a mirror to constantly check your posture, hand position and movement. Look at your stance and see if you are standing almost like a cat, with your back slightly hunched, chin lowered and your lead shoulder slightly up and prepared to spring. Contract your abdominal muscles partially. Protect your sides with your elbows and leave no openings at which your opponent may hit. The on-guard position is considered the safest stance. In jeet kune do, it is the most favorable position for kicking, hitting and applying bodily force.

Here are some faults on the following stances, as in photos A to O (see pages 26-31):

A: His right leg is too far out and will hinder his movement, especially with the weight on his rear foot. With both hands on his hips, he leaves himself wide open for an upper-body and head attack.

B: His stance is too square, and he can easily be thrown off-balance. He is also restricted from deep penetration in his countering.

C: His elongated stance with a long lead and an extended foot places him in a vulnerable position. The lead side of the body is open to attack, the extended hand is immobilized and withdrawing the hand telegraphs his intention.

D: Both his hands are too extended. His rear arm is held too high and leaves his body wide open. His front hand is too extended to deliver an attack.

E: Standing too much to the side prevents him from deep penetration while attacking or retreating. He can easily be thrown off-balance.

F: Both arms are carried too low, exposing his upper body and head.

G: His body is too rigid. The lead hand is too extended for attacking, and the rear hand is too low for protecting blows to the head.

H: His stance is too wide for any kind of mobility. It is difficult to attack without telegraphing from this position, and the groin area is exposed for a front kick.

I: His right arm is carried too high and leaves the rib-cage area exposed. His hand is too extended to deliver an attack.

J: The cat stance restricts movements, especially when side-stepping toward his right if he is in the right lead position. Secondly, any blow delivered from this position would not have power because his weight is fully on the rear foot.

K: His stance is too narrow. It eliminates the springiness of his footwork. The knees should be slightly bent for explosive and springy movement.

L: Like the cat stance, too much weight is placed on his back foot, and this restricts his forward mobility, especially with a wide stance. To launch a punch, he has to shift his weight to the front foot and telegraph his intention.

M: Too much weight on the lead foot could throw him off-balance by a sweep. A too-extended stance is also vulnerable for a kick to the knee and shin.

N: With both hands on the hips, his body and head are completely exposed for an assault. The groin area is unnecessarily open because of the awkward placement of his rear foot.

O: This stance makes the body, the face, and the knee and shin of the lead leg vulnerable. Kneeling on the floor just about eliminates any mobility for attack or defense.

Balance

Balance is the most important aspect of the on-guard stance. Without proper balance at all times, you will lose body control in the middle of an action. Balance is only attained with correct body alignment. Your feet should be directly under your body, spread apart at a comfortable medium distance (the space of a natural step) so you are braced and not standing on just one point. The weight of your body can be evenly balanced on both feet or slightly on your lead foot. By bending the forward knee, the center of gravity leans slightly forward, but the lead heel should have only light ground contact to retain balance and reduce tension ("light on your feet"). The lead leg should also be fairly straight with the knee, not locked but relaxed and loose. Although the above rule is generally true, there is no hard and

fast rule that your heels should constantly be raised or flat. This depends on the situation and position of your body.

The rear heel is raised to facilitate shifting your weight quickly to the lead leg when delivering a punch. It also acts as a spring to your body. It gives in when taking a blow. Like the lead knee, it should be slightly bent but relaxed and flexible when performing. A good fighter is rarely detected with his knee straight, even when he has to move suddenly.

The on-guard position presents a perfect body balance that should be constantly maintained. The lead side of the body creates a direct, imaginary line from the front heel to the tip of the front shoulder, as in photos 1 (front view) and 1A (bird's-eye view). In photo 2, the side view of Lee's position reveals the natural distance between the feet, both knees slightly bent, and the rear heel raised a bit more than the front.

This stance allows you several advantages: speed, relaxation, balance and smooth movement, plus it permits you to unleash a powerful blow.

Good balance is controlling your body in any position by controlling your center of gravity. Even if your body is slanted or is placed in an unstable equilibrium—away from the base of support— you should be able to pursue and recover your equilibrium.

In photo A, Lee retreats from his opponent, maintaining good balance, and in photo B, he throws a long punch but still controls his body for any countering attack.

To control the center of gravity in motion, take a short step and glide instead of a hop or cross-step. To move rapidly, take several small steps. Take two medium steps instead of one long stride to cover the same distance. Your center of gravity constantly changes according to your own actions and those of your opponent. For instance, to advance swiftly, the center of gravity should subtly be transferred to the lead or front foot, unrestraining the back foot to propel your body forward in a quick, short and sudden burst. To retreat or move back quickly, the center of gravity should be transferred to the back foot, allowing you to be in balance for a parry or a counterattack.

Wide strides or constant switching of weight from one foot to the other in your movement should be eliminated, except in hitting and kicking. That moment between shifting results in poor balance, places you in a position vulnerable to an attack and prevents you from launching a strong attack. Additionally, it allows the opponent to time his attack at the moment of shifting.

You should strive for good balance in motion and not only in stillness. You must attempt to control your body with perfect balance, especially while delivering effective punches and kicks, because you must shift your weight constantly from one foot to the other. Retaining your balance while constantly changing your body weight is an art few people ever master.

It is all right to switch your strategy while fighting or sparring, but don't stray far from your basic form. In photo 1, the figure

A

is in a fairly good position but with slightly too much weight on his front foot. But as soon as he attempts to launch an attack, as in photo 2 (see page 35), he throws himself out of balance. Good form requires good balance. Proper balance and perfect timing contribute to good leverage, which is necessary to kick or punch with sustained power.

The most ideal position of your feet is one that permits you to maneuver instantly in all directions and serves as a pivotal point for your entire attack. It keeps you in good balance to withstand blows from all sides and, at the same time, furnishes you with the ability to unleash unforeseen power in your blows. As in baseball, the drive and power in swinging a bat are also derived from your legs.

The on-guard position presents you with balance and ease of movement through proper body alignment. A too-wide stance, as in photo A, deviates from correct alignment. It provides sturdiness and power but forfeits speed and efficient movement. A short stance, as in photo B, presents speed but loses power and proper balance.

Do not overcommit in throwing a punch or a kick—it affects

your balance. Practice countering against a stand-up opponent. When he misses with a blow, he loses balance for an instant and is vulnerable to a counter. The only recourse he has, to be fairly safe, is to keep his knees slightly bent.

Learn kinesthetic perception, which is the faculty to feel muscle contraction and relaxation. The only way to develop this kinesthetic perception at first is to place your body and its parts in different positions and be highly sensitive about them. For example, place yourself in a balanced position and then an imbalanced one, feeling the contrast as you move forward, backward and to both sides. Once you have attained this feeling, use it as a constant guide to your body as it moves from gracefulness to awkwardness and from relaxation to tension. Finally, your kinesthetic perception should be so keen that you are uncomfortable unless your body functions with minimal effort to achieve maximum results.

To develop correct balance, practice from both the right and left stances, especially when performing the same tactics or exercises. Between training sessions, stand on one foot while putting on your clothes or shoes.

Practicing "chi sao" (sticky-hands exercise) is one of the best ways to develop balance. In the wing chun method, both practitioners keep their feet parallel to each other, as in photos 1 and 2. Both of their hands are extended until only their wrists touch each other. Each one, keeping one hand inside and the other outside of his opponent's hands, rotates his arms back and forth in a counterclockwise motion. Pressure should be applied to the arms in order to rock the partner from his position. To prevent this,

each should keep his knees slightly bent and keep the center of gravity downward by lowering his hips. In this position, you have good balance from side to side but not back and forth. Eventually, Lee converted the stance by placing one foot forward, as in photos 3 and 4. In this position, one has better all-around balance and better structure for applying energy. This modification is not quite the jeet kune do on-guard position, but it resembles it more closely. For more discussion on chi sao, go to page 70.

Chapter 3
Footwork

Footwork

In jeet kune do, mobility is heavily emphasized because hand-to-hand combat is a matter of movements. Your application of an effective technique depends on your footwork. Speed of your footwork leads the way for fast kicks and punches. If you are slow on your feet, you will be slow with your hands and feet, too.

The principle of fighting is the art of mobility: to seek your target or to avoid being a target. Footwork in jeet kune do should be easy, relaxed and alive but firm in movement, while the traditional, classical horse stance seeks solidity in stillness. This unnecessary, strenuous stance is not functional because it is slow and awkward. In fighting, you are required to move in any direction instantly.

Proper footwork is good balance in action, which contributes to hitting power and avoidance of punishment. Good footwork will beat any kick or punch. A moving target is definitely more difficult to hit than a stationary one. The more skillful you are with your footwork, the less you have to use your arms to block or parry kicks and punches. By moving deftly, you can elude almost any blow and, at the same time, prepare your fists and feet to attack.

Besides evading blows, footwork allows you to cover distance rapidly, escape out of a tight corner and conserve your energy to counter with more sting in your punch or kick. A heavy slugger with poor footwork will exhaust himself as he futilely attempts to hit his opponent.

Properly positioning your feet allows you to move rapidly in any direction and withstand blows from any angle. The feet must always be directly under your body. The on-guard stance presents proper body balance and a natural alignment of your feet.

The Shuffle

To advance, do not cross or hop but shuffle your feet. At the outset, you will feel clumsy and slow, but as you keep practicing this movement daily, you will develop your speed and grace. To do the forward shuffle, as in photos 1, 2 and 3 (front view), A, B and C (side view) and X, Y and Z (back view), stand in the on-guard position. To move forward cautiously, slide your front

ADVANCE SHUFFLE (Front View)

ADVANCE SHUFFLE (Side View)

ADVANCE SHUFFLE (Back View)

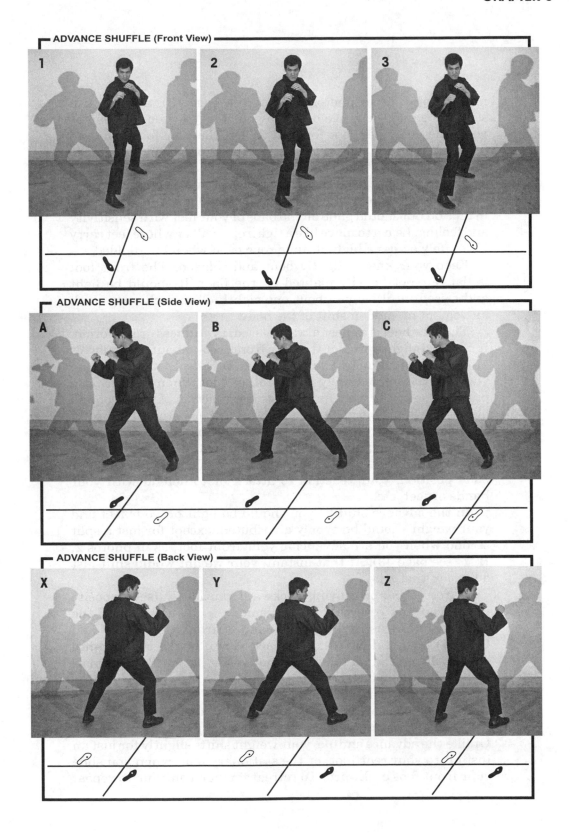

foot forward, as in photos 2, B, Y (see page 43), about a half step, widening the space between your feet just for a second as you slide your rear foot forward. When the rear foot is moved forward, you should be at the original position. Then, to advance farther forward, repeat the process.

Notice in the photos that Bruce Lee retains complete balance constantly and keeps his guard up. You should not be flat-footed in motion but should glide on the balls of your feet with sensitivity and feeling. Learn to move like a tightrope walker whose feet carry him safely across a high-altitude rope even when blindfolded.

Keep your knees slightly bent and relaxed. The front foot is flat but not heavily planted on the floor. It should be light and raised intuitively—about one-eighth of an inch on a quick movement or sudden shift of the body.

The rear heel is almost always raised, in stillness or in motion. It is raised slightly higher than the front foot—about one-quarter or one-half of an inch. The raised rear heel facilitates switching your weight immediately to the other foot when delivering a punch. The raised back heel allows fast reaction of that foot and also acts as a spring, giving in to blows from any angle. Naturally, the heel should drop at the impact of the blow. There is no hard and fast rule that your heels should be constantly raised or that they should be flat. This depends on several factors, such as your body position, your reaction to attack or to defend with your hands or feet, etc.

In the advance shuffle, you should be light on your feet and your weight should be evenly distributed, except for just a split second when you are advancing your front foot, as in photos 2, B, Y (see page 43). At that instant, your weight would shift just a little to that foot.

In retreating or moving backward cautiously (see opposite page), you just reverse your movement. The basis behind the retreat shuffle, as in photos 1, 2 and 3 (front view), A, B and C (side view) and X, Y and Z (back view), is like the advance shuffle. From the on-guard position, slide or shuffle your rear foot backward about a half step, as in photos 2, B and Y, widening the space between your feet just for a split second as you slide your front foot backward. When the front foot is in place, you should be in the on-guard position and perfectly balanced. Unlike the advance shuffle, your weight shifts slightly for just an instant to your rear foot, or the stationary foot, when you slide your front foot backward. To retreat farther, continue to repeat

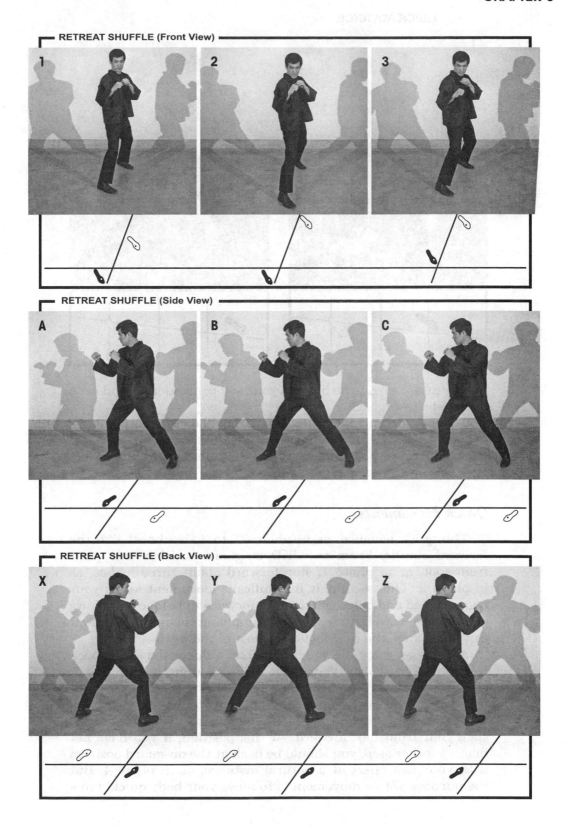

QUICK ADVANCE

the process. Learn to be light on your feet continuously and keep your rear heel raised.

The forward and backward shuffle must be made with a series of short steps to retain complete balance. This position prepares you to shift your body quickly to any direction, and it is a perfect position for attacking or defending.

Quick Movements

The quick advance, as in photos 1 to 4, is almost like the forward shuffle. From the JKD on-guard position with your front foot, as in photo 1, step forward about three inches, as in photo 2. This seemingly insignificant movement keeps your body aligned and helps you to move forward in balance. It allows you to move with both feet evenly supplying the power. Without this short step, the rear foot does most of the work.

As soon as you glide your front foot, quickly slide your back foot almost to replace your front foot's position, as in photo 3. Unless you move your front foot instantly, the rear foot cannot be planted properly because the front foot will be partially in its way. So just before your rear foot makes contact with your front, slide your front foot forward. At this position, if you have not taken another step, you should be back at the on-guard position with your feet apart at a natural distance, as in photo 4. But the purpose of this movement is to move your body quickly to a

distance, eight feet or more, that requires several steps. Except for the first three-inch step, the series of steps should be made at a normal walking space. This movement keeps your body in perfect alignment and allows you to move rapidly ahead.

In photo 3, it seems like Lee is in an awkward position, but he is in that position for just a split second. If you were actually watching him physically, you would have witnessed only a flowing, graceful movement and never would have detected any awkwardness.

Quick Retreat

The footwork for the quick retreat or rapid backward movement is similar to the quick advance, except you move in the opposite direction. From the on-guard position, move your front foot back, as in photos A and B (see page 48). The front foot, like the quick advance, initiates the movement with the rear foot following just a split second later. Unless you move your rear foot before the front foot makes contact, the front foot cannot be planted properly. Unlike the quick advance, you do not have to slide your foot three inches. It is just one quick motion, but your body should be in alignment and in balance. If you were to move just once, you should be at the on-guard position when both of your feet are in place. But the purpose of this movement is to move your body four feet or more.

The quick movement and shuffle can only be accomplished

QUICK RETREAT

by being light on your feet. The best exercise for overcoming the force of inertia on your feet is skipping rope and shadowboxing several minutes. While exercising, you must constantly be conscious of keeping your feet "light as a feather." Eventually, you will be stepping around with natural lightness.

You must move without any strain, gliding on the balls of your feet, bending your knees slightly, and keeping your rear heel raised. Have feeling or sensitivity in your footwork. Quick or relaxed footwork is a matter of proper balance. In your training, as you return to an on-guard position, as in photo C, after each phase of maneuvers, shuffle on the balls of your feet with ease and feeling before continuing to your next maneuver. This drill enhances your skill as it simulates actual fighting.

Unless there is a strategic purpose, forward and backward movements should be made with short and quick slides. Lengthy steps or foot actions, which cause your weight to shift from one foot to the other, should be eliminated except in delivering a blow because, at that moment, your body is imbalanced—restricting your attack or defense effectively. Crossing your feet in motion is a bad habit because it tends to unbalance you and exposes your groin area.

The movement should not be a series of hops, nor should it be jerky. Both feet should slither rhythmically just above the surface of the floor like a graceful ballroom dancer. Visually, your movement should not be like the kangaroo hopping across the open plain but like the stallion galloping with even, rhythmic and graceful strokes of his feet.

The Burst

The forward burst or lunge is the quickest JKD movement. It is also one of the hardest to learn because it depends on good coordination and because your balance can be thrown off very easily. It is utilized to penetrate deeply to attack with a side kick or to counter an attack such as a kick.

The forward burst is one deep lunge. From an on-guard position, as in photo 1, step forward about three inches with your front foot, like the quick advance movement, to align your body and be in balance, as in photo 2. Then, for faster reaction,

use your lead hand as an impetus. By sweeping your lead hand upward, a momentum is created, like someone is jerking you forward suddenly as you are holding on to a rope, as in drawings A and B. This sweep of your hand also distracts your opponent and throws his timing off.

While sweeping your hand upward, your hips swing forward simultaneously, dragging your rear foot forward. In that split instant, your weight is heavily on your front foot, only at this moment your leg straightens out to thrust your body forward. Sometimes, on an especially deep, penetrating leap, your rear foot may be ahead of your front foot while you are gliding in the air, as in photo X. You must land on your left foot only as your right foot is delivering a side kick, as in photo Y. As soon as you have completed your kick, you should quickly place your right foot down and assume the on-guard position. That one leap should carry your body at least two wide steps.

In a recently conducted test, by using the forward burst, it took only three-quarters of a second to travel eight feet. By applying the classical lunge movement or stepping by crossing your feet, it took one-and-one-half seconds to reach the same distance—twice the time.

The leap should be more horizontal than vertical. It is more like a broad jump than a high jump. You should try for distance by keeping your feet close to the floor. Your knees should always be bent slightly so that the powerful thigh muscles' springy explosiveness is utilized.

When practicing this footwork in the beginning, don't worry about your hands. Just keep them in the regular JKD position and concentrate on your footwork. Once you are accustomed to the feet movement with proper balance, learn to sweep your hand forward just before each leap.

Later, to develop speed and naturalness in your movement,

adopt the following exercise in your daily training. From an on-guard position, do the forward burst without penetrating too deeply by sweeping your hand upward, leaping forward without straining yourself and quickly placing your front foot down without kicking. Continue to do this motion over and over again without stopping, but keep your balance and fluidity in motion. This exercise is excellent to adapt your body to move with ease, rhythm and grace. As you become more adapted to the movement, increase your speed and work toward shortening the distance between you and your opponent by more and more execution. Eventually, you can substitute a backfist punch for the sweeping movement of your hand.

The backward burst is like the quick backward movement except that it carries your body backward more quickly and deeply. From an on-guard position, push the ball of your front foot to initiate the motion, which straightens your front knee and shifts the weight to the rear foot. Then the front foot, without pausing from the initial motion, leaves the floor and crosses your rear foot. Just before it lands, your rear leg, with its knee bent and acting like a spring, should thrust your body with a sudden straightening of its leg. You should land on the ball of your front foot just a second before your rear foot touches the floor. That one quick motion should carry your body backward at least two natural walking steps.

The backward burst carries your body just as fast as the forward lunge. In the same test (see page 50), it took exactly the same time to travel eight feet backward as forward—three-quarters of a second. By comparison, the classical movement covered the same distance in one second flat.

For your daily training, do the backward burst for speed, balance and rhythm instead of deep penetration. Move with lightness of your feet and keep practicing toward shortening the distance. You can also do isometric exercises to build up your calves to help with your burst for speed, as in photo 1.

While jogging, do a quick advance by rapidly shuffling your feet and then returning to your jogging. Another exercise is to practice with a partner. Let your partner do the backward burst while you do the forward burst. From an on-guard position, attempt to reach your partner with a light side kick as he tries to keep his distance. Then, reverse your positions.

Learn not to hurl yourself recklessly at your partner but attempt to narrow the gap of space in a calm and exact manner. Keep drilling faster and faster by lunging two to three hundred times per day. Acceleration can be increased only by discipline in your workout.

Side Stepping

Side stepping is the technique of moving your body toward the right or left without losing your balance. It is a safe and essential defensive maneuver to attack or produce openings for a counter when the opponent least expects it. It is used to avoid straightforward assaults, blows or kicks. You can also frustrate your opponent by simply moving when he is about to attack.

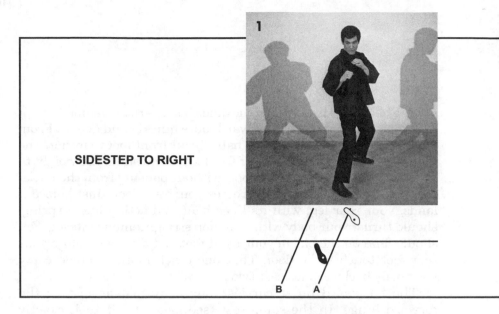

SIDESTEP TO RIGHT

To sidestep to the right from an unorthodox (southpaw) on-guard position, move your right foot slightly forward and sharply toward the right about 18 inches, as in photos 1 and 2. Your left or rear foot supplies the impetus as you land lightly on the ball of your right foot. For a split instant, your shoulder sways toward your right, and your weight shifts on the front foot with its knee bent. Your shoulder automatically realigns when you quickly slide your left foot in the exact same manner and resume the on-guard position, as in photo 3.

To sidestep to the left from a southpaw stance, as in photo A, move your left foot slightly forward and to your left about 18 inches, as in photo B. During this motion, your body is more

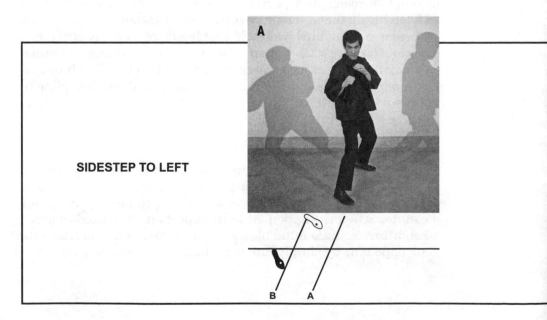

SIDESTEP TO LEFT

aligned than when moving toward the right. Because your body is more aligned, you are in better balance and your weight is evenly distributed between your two feet during the shift. Your right or front foot should follow immediately in the exact same manner, returning you to the on-guard stance, as in photo C. You will notice that sidestepping toward your left is more natural and easier than to the right.

Bruce Lee uses a staff to practice his footwork. In photo A (see page 56), he places the staff near his neck and slightly above his shoulder. The partner attempts to thrust the long staff at that exact area, and Lee adjusts to the thrust by using footwork.

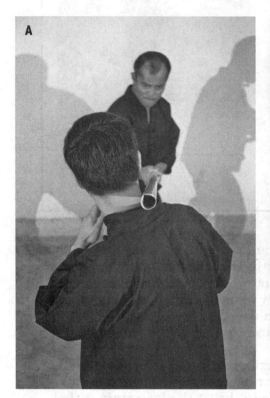

In photos B and C (front view), the partner thrusts his staff and Lee sidesteps toward his left, keeping his body in balance and his eyes continuously on his partner. He has to move sharply to avoid the edge of the staff.

In close fighting or infighting, a fairly safe stance is the drop shift or the forward drop, as in photo D. This is done by shifting your body forward and slightly to your left, with your head in close and both hands carried high. It is used to gain the outside or inside guard position, which enables you to strike the opponent's groin, throw an uppercut, stomp his instep or grapple him down. In the forward shift, you can move directly to the left, right or back, using the same step. This depends on your strategy and the degree of safety required in that instant.

Against an orthodox fighter, you would sidestep to your right or away from his rear hand. Against a southpaw, you move the opposite way, meaning mostly to your left. The art of side stepping

is not to move early but late and quickly, just before you are hit.

In nearly all motions, your first step is with the foot moving to that particular direction in which you intend to go. In other words, if you sidestep to your right, your right foot moves first toward that direction. If you sidestep to your left, your left foot moves first.

To move quickly, your body should lean toward the direction you are going just before you step out.

In jeet kune do, the aim of footwork is simplification, economy and speed with a minimum of motion. Move just enough to avoid the opponent's attack or blow, and let him commit himself fully. Do not tire yourself by dancing on your toes like a fancy boxer.

While practicing, stand naturally—with ease and comfort—so your muscles can perform at their peak. Learn to differentiate between personal comfort and drilling comfort. You should never be set or tense but flexible and prepared.

CHAPTER 4
Power Training

Power Training

Power in hitting is not based strictly on strength. How many times have you seen a boxer who is not muscular but packs a wallop in his punch? And then you see another heavily muscular boxer who can't knock anyone down. The reason behind this is that power isn't generated by your contractile muscles but from the impetus and speed of your arm or foot. Bruce Lee, a 130-pounder, was able to hit harder than a man twice his size because Lee's blow, with a heavy force behind it, was much faster.

In jeet kune do, you do not hit by just swinging your arm. Your whole body should participate in the impetus—your hips, shoulders, feet and arms. The inertia of your punch should be a straight line in front of your nose—using it as the guiding point—as in photo 1. The punch originates not from the shoulder but from the center of your body.

In photo 2, the fist lands too far to his left, exposing his right side for a counterattack and not allowing much time to recover for a defense. In photo 3, the punch comes from his shoulder with not much power behind it. He is too rigid to take advantage of his hip and body motion.

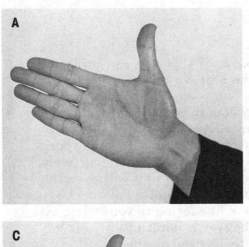

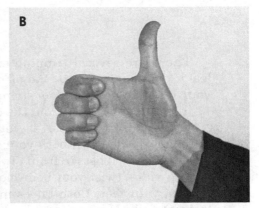

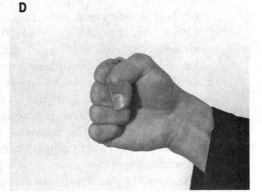

Punching Power

Straight punching or kicking is the basis for scientific and artistic fighting. It is a modern concept in fisticuffs derived from the knowledge of body leverage and makeup. A punch from your arm alone doesn't supply enough power. Your arms should be used strictly as bearers of your force, and the correct application of your body should furnish the power. In any power punching, the body must be balanced and aligned with your lead foot, forming a straight line. This section of your body is the mainstay, functioning as an axis to generate power.

Before you can punch with power, you must first learn to clench your fists properly—otherwise, you are liable to injure them. From an outspread position of your fingers and thumb, as in photo A, roll your fingertips into your palm, as in photos B and C. Then overlap your thumb tightly over your clenched fingers. The tip of the thumb extends to the center of your middle finger, as in photo D.

There are several training exercises that you can utilize to learn power punching. One of the best ways is to learn to use your hips. To do this, tie a string to a piece of paper, about 8 by 11 inches, and hang it from the ceiling to your chest height.

Using this thin paper as your target, stand about seven to ten inches away with both your feet parallel to it. Keeping both loosely clenched fists in front of your chest, elbows hanging freely at your sides, twist your body clockwise as far as it will go on the balls of your feet. Both knees must bend slightly for your body to twist fully. Now, your body should be facing to your right, 90 degrees from the target, with the weight shifting to your left foot. But your eyes must constantly be fixed on the target.

Pivot on the balls of your feet, with your hips initiating a sudden, rotating motion. Your weight quickly shifts to your other foot as your shoulders automatically rotate after your hips. Simultaneously, as your body is rotating, raise your right elbow to your shoulder height just in time to apply an elbow strike to the proper target. The momentum should turn your body 180 degrees so it faces the opposite or left side. It is very important that your hips rotate slightly ahead of your shoulders to obtain maximum power.

Repeat the same motion from the left side, striking with your left elbow. Once you have learned to control your body and begin to feel at ease in this exercise, you may use your fists.

Step back about 20 to 25 inches from the target. Keeping your exact body position, swing at the target with a straight punch. At this point, your body should be aligned properly, you should have good balance and your motion should be fluid, with your hips initiating the rotation. Your power in the punches should increase between 80 percent to 100 percent.

Gradually, to keep your body in balance, especially after the completion of the swing, place your left foot forward and your right foot back (orthodox stance). From this position, twist your body clockwise until your shoulders are in a straight line with the target. Your front foot should be about 15 inches away. Now your weight leans heavily on your rear foot with both knees slightly bent. As the hips initiate the movement, you pivot on the balls of both feet, and your body is driven forward by the impetus from the rear foot. Your rear heel rises as your weight quickly shifts to the front foot with the delivery of the punch. At the completion of the action, your rear knee is practically straightened and your rear heel is almost completely raised. Your body should be facing the target. This motion is similar to a baseball player swinging a bat with all his might.

Once you have grasped this way of hitting, you can begin to work on your power blows by hitting the heavy punching bag, as in photo A. Here, Lee uses his elbow strike to develop his hip motion, then later works on his punches, as in photo B.

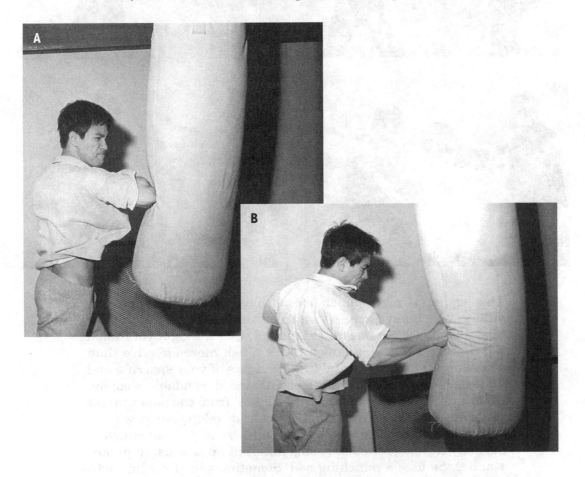

Your final step in punching for power is to reverse your footing and position yourself in the on-guard stance, with your right foot in front. With both of your knees slightly bent and rear heel raised, shift your weight just slightly to the rear foot for an instant. Your weight should be set for less than a second because you have to rotate your hips counterclockwise and because your weight switches to the front foot just before you throw a punch.

This leading straight punch doesn't have as much power as the others, which have access to a freer and fuller rotation of the hips. But if you can master this punch with the right rotational hip timing, you have a punch that's much more effective than a jab and very instrumental in the success of your sparring and fighting. It will be your most usable and dependable weapon. Like with the other punching techniques, from the paper target you can substitute more solid targets to develop your power.

Lee used to concentrate heavily on the straight lead punch in his daily training schedule, using different apparatus. In photos 1 and 2, he uses a punching pad. Sometimes he drew his right hand back to throw a much heavier blow, as in photos 3 and 4 to simulate close fighting.

Another apparatus used in his training was the light shield, as in photos X and Y. Lee liked to use various hitting equipment. He used to say, "I don't know the true feeling of hitting a person. First of all, each part of the human body has a different composition. You may hit a hard, bony substance or a soft, fatty

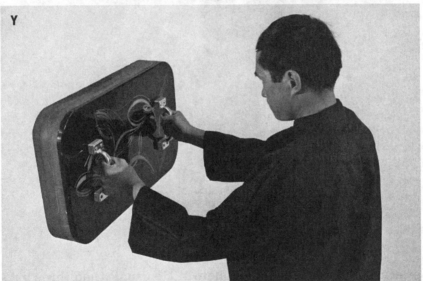

area. And second, hitting with gloves on is different from bare knuckles. Unfortunately, using bare knuckles on your partner is not too practical."

The shield presents a different feeling when there is contact. The shield is more solid than the pad, and because the holder stands more firmly with both hands on the equipment, it will not give in like the pad will. For a more punishing punch, Lee

selects the canvas bag, as in photo 1. He usually had three bags hanging on the wall. One was filled with sand, another with gravel or beans and the third with steel sawdust found in any machine shop. In the beginning, it is wise that you wear light boxing gloves on the heavy canvas bag as well as these wall bags. You must first toughen your knuckles before going bare-fisted.

In jeet kune do, your punches are not thrown like the classical stylist's. Instead of using the first two knuckles (the index and the middle fingers), use the last three knuckles, as in photo 2.

The punches are not thrown from the hips in jeet kune do like the person on the left is doing in photos A and B, but rather they are thrown from the chest, as Lee is about to do in photo A. The delivery should be straight and not with a twist of your hand. If you twist your hand, the knuckles will align horizontally at impact, but if you deliver straight out, it will hit the target either vertically or obliquely, as in photo B. Consequently, you should toughen the last three knuckles, as in photo 2.

Besides punching the wall canvas bags for toughening, you can also train with a sand or gravel box, as in photo C. Other exercises include push-ups with your clenched fists. Place the knuckles of your index fingers and the two small fingers on a hard floor so your palms face each other. This is an excellent exercise for beginners because they can gradually toughen their knuckles without risk of injury.

By being in the southpaw or JKD on-guard position, it is apparent that the right or lead hand will lose considerable punching power to a right-hander. Unless he can draw his right hand farther back, he lacks the space needed to deliver the most devastating blow. Power is now being replaced by speed in this case. To compensate, the left or rear hand must do the job.

If you are a natural right-hander, punching with the left seems very awkward in the beginning. You'll be off-balance, and your punch from that hand will be weak, slow and not too accurate. But by constantly practicing with your right foot as the lead, as in photo A, and doing the motion exactly, you should develop your punching power in that hand.

Eventually, your rear straight punch and cross will be the most powerful punches available in your arsenal. You will be depending on them for your knockout blows. Keep practicing with your left hand until it becomes natural.

One of the most helpful but simple implements that Bruce Lee incorporated into his training schedule was the round steel cylinder. The cylinder, weighing about a pound, fits snugly in the hand. You can quickly improve your delivery of punches by taking advantage of this exercise. Holding one of these cylinders in each hand, stand with your feet parallel and punch directly in front of your nose several times. The idea behind this is to develop the snapping or whipping blows. If you keep your body and arms relaxed, you will notice that your punches will automatically snap back at the end of your delivery.

This training has a twofold purpose. It develops speed in your delivery as well as in your power. After a while you will learn to punch with heaviness in your blows even without the weights. The secret behind the exercise is to concentrate or pretend that your empty hands still contain the cylinders as you throw the punches.

In throwing a hard punch, it is easy to develop the bad habit of throwing your shoulders out of line so only one shoulder does the work. In other words, the alignment of the shoulders can easily be disturbed, causing loss of power in delivery. To retain the coordination between the shoulders, Lee uses a staff, as in photos 1 and 2. By holding the staff with his hands far apart, he places it on his back shoulders. As he twists his body from one position to another, the long staff keeps his shoulders straight in all the movements.

After you have practiced with the cylinder weights for some time, you will notice that your blows have more impact even without the weights. This is your introduction to the fact that your mind can do wonders to your physical strength. This extra power or strength is what Lee called "flowing energy," which in aikido is called "ki" and in tai chi chuan is called "chi."

What you are now experiencing is just a small degree of flowing energy. To enhance this energy, there are several exercises, and one of the best exercises that should be an integral part of your training is the chi sao, which was briefly described in Chapter 2.

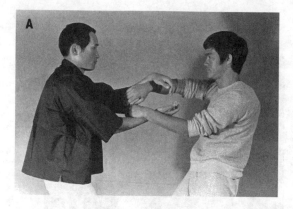

In performing chi sao to develop your energy, keep your body and arms relaxed, as in photos 1 to 6 (bird's-eye view) and photos A and B (side view). As your wrists touch your partner's, as in figure A, just put enough stress in your hands to roll your arms back and forth. In photos 1 to 6, Lee demonstrates how your arms should be rolling. Arrows are indicated in each photo to illustrate the motion of the hands. The elbows are positioned close to the body as they roll their arms constantly and smoothly. Though the arms appear to roll from side to side, the concentration of your energy should be forward.

The rolling motion is not the essence of chi sao. It is the flowing from your arms that is important. The idea in the early stages is not to fight each other's strength but to concentrate on getting the feel of this energy. If you attempt to shove your partner backward, you will be missing the whole purpose of chi sao. This forceful movement will tense your arms, and consequently, your shoulders will become rigid. You will then lose your balance and begin to rely on brute strength instead of the flowing energy. Think of a screw that is turning inward. You never unwind the screw; you keep a small area inside and always drive it forward.

This energy must flow from the pit of your abdomen instead of your shoulders. To do this, imagine that water is flowing through your arms like a hose being fed from the center of your body from about the navel. This causes the under part of your arms to become heavy. Keep your fingers loose and outstretched because the water has to flow out from the little fingers.

If both partners emit the same degree of energy or "water" through their arms, neither will penetrate the other. The motion

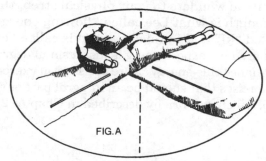

FIG. A

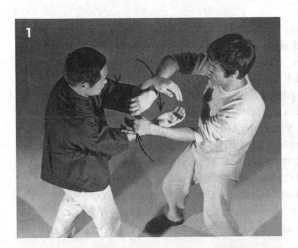

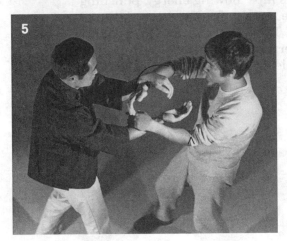

will be constant, even and rhythmic. Each partner will feel the other's arms as supple but firm. Arms look weak, but they are very potent. Your elbows should be immovable—they can't be coerced toward your body. Your pliable arms can be moved from side to side but not toward your body. As you become more proficient, the circumference of your motion or rolling becomes smaller and smaller, as if the water flowing through your arms is now trying to penetrate and cover all the smaller cracks.

Chi sao is an important part of jeet kune do because its efficient application of techniques relies on the looseness of the arms and body. This exercise is the best way to develop your flowing energy so you can be constantly relaxed and loose but not sacrifice power.

To test if your energy is flowing, have someone extend his hand to you, then land a chopping blow to his hand. First, do it normally and then do it with the flowing energy—concentrate on the heaviness of your hand, keep your arm loose and place the weight at the bottom of your arm. Don't tell your partner what you are doing. After each blow, ask him whether he feels any difference. If he does, then hit his hand both with and without the flowing energy, letting him decide after each blow whether the force is heavier or lighter. If the blows with the flowing energy are more powerful, you know you are doing it right. If you are unable to find anyone to cooperate with you, you can also test it on your own hand.

The incredible one-inch punch, as in photos 1, 2 and 3, which Lee used to awe crowds with at demonstrations, was possible because of his proficient use of his hips, flowing energy, punching through and the delivering of the punch. The fist is vertical and cocked at the wrist, as in photo A. The fist turns upward suddenly at impact, as in photo B. This vertical-fist punch is only used in close quarters from five inches or less to the target. If you attempt

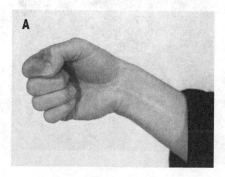
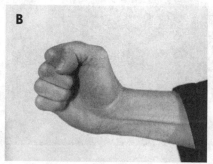

to use this punch from a distance, it will throw your timing off at impact. The one-inch punch is really more for demonstration purposes. Generally, you never want to bend your wrist in a real fighting situation because you may injure yourself.

There are other ways to amplify the power of your flowing energy. You can do it while driving your car. Place your arms on the steering wheel as if you are doing chi sao and put pressure on your arms. In photo A, it seems like Lee is doing isometric exercises, but he is actually pressing his arms to the bar, flowing his energy. Fortunately, developing your flowing energy can be practiced anywhere that allows you to put pressure on one or both arms.

Many who attempt the one-inch punch knock their opponents off their feet, but instead of punching, they only push them down. You can't hurt your opponent by a push. The art of punching is not pushing. In punching, the peak of your force or strength is at the point of contact, but in pushing, the force begins from the outset of the delivery and generally loses its power by the time your arm is fully extended. Punching comes from the rotation of your hips, while pushing is usually from the rear foot, propelling your body forward.

When you are hitting, especially the heavy bag, punch through the bag. You will find that you will have a deeper and stronger penetration if you do that instead of concentrating on the surface of the bag. "Follow-through" means continuous acceleration of your punch to the target. However, the momentum or power does not cease there but extends through the target. It isn't hitting your opponent but driving through him. After driving through him, your punching hand should be withdrawn as quickly as you thrust it forward.

Don't throw your punches in a windup motion; they should be thrown straight. Your fist clenches just before your whip-like impact. To add additional power, the free hand can be drawn suddenly and conjunctly toward your body at the point of impact.

If you are taking a step to throw a punch, your fist makes the contact before your foot lands on the floor; otherwise, the body weight would be assimilated onto the floor instead of behind your punch. Your hips and shoulders must initiate the action before your arm to deliver a rapid, precise and powerful blow. Although your foot movement adds to your power, you can actually knock out your opponent without taking a step or showing any strain in your action, if delivery is correctly done.

A powerful blow depends on leverage and timing. Right timing is a must for a powerful blow. Without it, your impact is lost in motion—it may reach too early or too late.

Pulling Power

Although Bruce Lee first studied wing chun kung fu, he improvised so many different techniques that jeet kune do seems to have no bearing on kung fu. Lee did not completely discard wing chun's techniques. He retained some of them but also altered them so completely that they are not recognizable as the original art.

Two techniques he continued to practice were "lop sao" (grabbing the hand) and "pak sao" (slapping block), especially after doing chi sao. He was forced to revise both techniques because in wing chun both partners stand with their bodies facing each other squarely and with their feet parallel. But in the JKD on-guard position, the partners stand with one foot forward, and the hand extension is not the same.

Lee always believed that correct weight training could increase his power. But he was very selective in his exercise. He avoided drills that would develop muscles that would interfere with his performance in sparring or fighting.

Besides the abdominal muscles, he concentrated heavily on his forearms because he believed they were the muscles depended on in punching and in pulling, as in lop sao. His drills included the reverse curl. To receive the most benefit from this, he covered the bar with a sponge so he lost his gripping power as he wrapped his hands over the sponge. When doing the exercise, he depended heavily on his forearm muscles to carry the weights to his chest.

Another excellent exercise for the forearms was the reverse extension. Instead of curling his arms, he lifted the weights straight out in front of him. With his arms fully extended, he supported the weights for as long as possible at chest level.

He also squeezed a rubber ball in his palm and worked with the wrist roller, as in photos 1 and 2. Using the dumbbell without the plates on one end, he twisted his wrist back and forth.

Lee developed such strength in his arms that when he jerked his partner, he snapped his head backward as the body flew toward him. A contributing factor that developed the pulling power was his persistent training of lop sao on the wing chun "dummy," as in photo A. Besides developing the forearm muscles, he toughened

his arms by slamming them into the wooden arm.

While working out with weights, be sure to include speed and flexibility exercises congruently. A heavy weightlifter with a great deal of power but no flexibility or speed will have a problem hitting his opponent. It will be like a rhinoceros trying to corner a rabbit.

Power Kicking

Striking with your foot has several advantages. First, your leg is much more powerful than your hand. Actually, kicking properly is the most powerful and damaging blow you can administer. Second, your leg is longer than your hand, so it is your first line of attack, normally preceding your punch. Third, blocking a kick is very difficult, especially on the low-line areas like the shin, knee and groin.

A

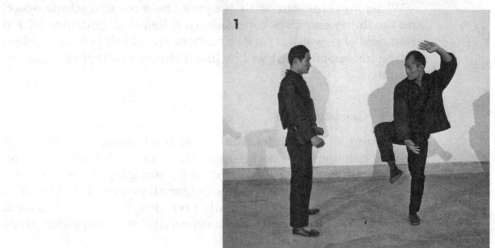

1

Unfortunately, too many martial artists do not profit from their assets. They do kick but without any power. Flicky or pole-like kicks, as in photos 1 to 3, are still being used. They do not generate enough power to hurt or damage. In the flicky kicks, your weight is not behind the blow, and in the polelike kicks, your body is too off-balance.

Bruce Lee's forte was the side kick, as shown in photo A, which differs from the classical side kick. In the classical, the side thrust kick has power but no speed. The side snap kick has speed but no power. In jeet kune do's side kick, both the snap and thrust are combined so there is no loss of power and speed. Lee used to drop a two-inch board from shoulder height and shatter it in half before it landed on the ground. If his kick had only power but no snap, the board would be hurled a distance without breaking, unless it was braced. If his kick had the snap but no power, the board would not break because a two-inch board without support is too thick to split with a snap kick.

To do the side kick, stand with your feet apart and parallel to each other. Lift your right foot about 12 inches from the floor as you balance on your left. Stomp your right foot straight down with force and let it snap upward about an inch from the floor. Like punching with flowing energy, here again, you should concentrate with heaviness in your foot. In other words, the water is now flowing through your right leg (hose), and when it is fully extended by your downward stomp (gushing of the water), it snaps upward (splashes explosively). Until you warm

up your legs by light kicking, do not stomp your foot violently.

Now you are set to kick sideways. As in stomping, place all your weight on your left foot as you lift your right foot and kick straight out instead of down. Your left knee should be bent slightly so you can lean a little backward and not forward, like most beginners do. Pivot on the ball of your left foot as you thrust your right foot forward. For extra power, twist your hips just an instant before the full extension of your leg—it gives you the screwdriver or the twisting force in your kick. Then snap your foot at the full extension for the whipping effect.

If you like to kick something solid, you can hit any wood or concrete wall. Measure your distance to the wall and just kick it. Because your foot should be landing flat, you will not hurt yourself. A forceful kick will just bounce your body backward because the wall will not flex.

After you have the knack of doing the side kick, you are prepared to kick the heavy bag. From the on-guard position, do the forward burst, as explained in Chapter 3. Aim your blow directly at the center of the bag, as in photos 1, 2 and 3.

At impact, your foot should land horizontally on the bag and not obliquely. The sound at impact should be a loud, cracking thud like a whip if you have kicked through the bag and snapped your foot at the end. If there is more push than hit, the sound will be a light or weak thud. In both kicks, force is exerted, except the hit will do the damage and the push will just knock the opponent down innocuously.

If you lunge at the bag swiftly and keep your body in balance, you can generate more power in your kick than you ever thought possible. Generally, the kick is delivered with your body lunging close to the floor to keep you in balance even after the execution. But for a much more powerful blow, lift your body a little higher while moving toward the bag, and just as you are propelling your right foot through the bag, stomp or drive your left foot downward. In other words, the force is now being exerted from both legs. This may be the way of delivering a punishing blow without a weapon.

One note of caution: If you miss the bag completely or don't hit it solidly, you can hurt your kicking knee. The reason is that your foot is hurling much faster than your body, and when you miss, it is like someone jerking your leg out of the knee socket.

In real fighting or sparring, it is not too practical to utilize the

latter kick because it can easily leave you off-balance if you miss. Furthermore, the higher you leap, the more time you allow your opponent to avoid your attack.

The heavy bag is one of the most valuable apparatuses in jeet kune do and, as a matter of fact, in the other martial arts, too, because one can practice on it alone. You can have a good workout by just doing the side kicks on it continuously for several minutes. As you kick the bag, let it swing back each time before kicking it again.

To teach a beginner in kicking, hold the bag for him by placing your knee at the bottom rim of the bag and both your hands gently behind the center area of the bag to avoid having your fingers crushed. Before you ever stand with your back facing the bag, be sure you know the strength of the kicker. In photo 1, Lee hit the bag so hard that the impact sent the person behind it flying across the room, causing an injury to his neck that lasted for several days from the whiplash.

Lee always believed that you should practice hitting different types of targets to get a different feeling from each on impact. He used the heavy bag mostly, but he often kicked at the wall canvas, beanbag or sandbag, the punching pad, the wooden dummy as in photo A, and the portable heavy shield as in photo B.

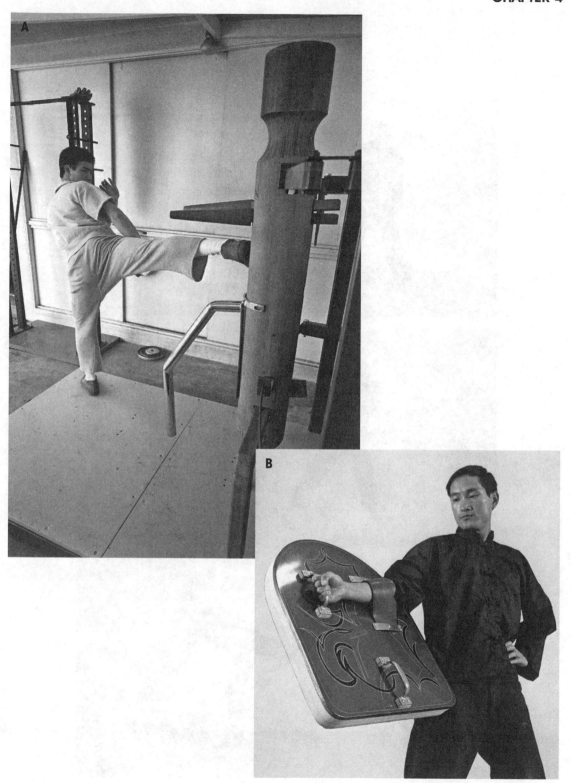

After the heavy bag, Lee's next favorite apparatuses to kick were the heavy shield and the air bag because he could exert all his power onto a moving target without really hurting the holder, as in photos 1, 2 and 3.

Although the front kick is not as powerful as the side kick, Lee increased the explosiveness of his kick by the use of his hips. Instead of relying only on the snap of the foot from the knee, he jerked his hips forward just an instant before his foot made contact, as in photos A and B. The timing of this movement is very important and difficult to do. Practice it daily until you have the knack of it.

The text attempts to illustrate a step-by-step instruction of doing the side kick. But once you understand how to deliver it, you should do it without hesitation but in one smooth, fluid motion.

CHAPTER 5
Speed Training

Speed Training

What is speed in fighting? Is it the velocity of your hands, feet and body movement? Or are there other, more prevalent essentials in a good fighter? What is a good fighter?

To answer these questions: A good fighter is a person who can hit his opponent quicker, harder, without much perceptible effort and yet avoid being hit. He doesn't only possess a pair of fast hands and feet or quick body movements but has other qualities such as nontelegraphic moves, good coordination, perfect balance and keen awareness. Although some people are endowed with a few of these qualities, most of these attributes are developed through hard training.

All the strength or power you have developed from your training is wasted if you are slow and can't make contact. Power and speed go hand in hand. A fighter needs both to be successful.

One immediate way to increase your speed at impact is to "snap" or "whip" your hand or foot just before contact. It is the same principle as the overhand throw. For example, if you throw a baseball by fully swinging your arm and snapping your wrist at the last moment or at the tail end of your swing, the ball will have more velocity than without the snap. Naturally, the longer swing with a snap will have more acceleration at the end than a shorter swing with a snap. A 12-foot whip, flung exactly, will generate more sting than a two-foot whip.

Speed in Punching

The backfist punch is neither the quickest nor is it very strong because you are unable to utilize the total body movement. But it is one blow in which you can fully apply the whipping or snapping motion. First, it is thrown more like a swing than a forward thrust, which means you can put more momentum in the delivery. Second, there is more elasticity or freedom of motion in your wrist when bending it from side to side (palm to knuckles) rather than up and down (thumb to little finger). That means you are able to whip or snap it more vigorously, as in photo A.

The backfist is used mostly to strike the head section of your opponent. It is used heavily in combination with lop sao (grabbing-the-hand technique), as in photo B. It is delivered at shoulder height, but it can also be used as a surprise attack and

be launched anywhere from your waistline to your shoulder. It is very difficult to block once you have acquired the nontelegraphic moves.

Although some power is lost in this punch, it is compensated for or redeemed when combined with lop sao. If you can develop a strong pulling power in your arm, you will be able to jerk your opponent forward and apply the backfist punch. The impact should be devastating when your knuckles hit your opponent's face. It is like two fast-moving cars colliding, head-on.

To develop speed or quickness in the backfist punch, light a candle and attempt to blow it out with the acceleration of your punch. Another interesting exercise is to have a partner attempt to block your punch as you throw it at his face, with control. If

he misses his block, you should be able to stop your punch about one-quarter inch from his skin.

Lee also used the bouncing head dummy, as in photo X, which was created strictly for solitary training. The head is padded and resilient to take hard blows.

The leading finger jab is the fastest attacking weapon available to you. It is fast in reaching your target because it travels only a short distance. It is also the longest hand weapon accessible to you. Because you do not clench your fist but have your fingers extended, you add several more inches to your reach, as in photos 1 and 2.

Power is not needed in this technique because you focus your aim at the eyes of your enemy. Instead, your important assets are accuracy and speed. The jab is a threatening and dangerous weapon to the adversary because it does so much damage and is so difficult to defend against.

To protect yourself from damaging your fingers, if you should ever miss and hit a hard object such as the head or a bone of your enemy, learn to form your hand properly. Align the tip of your hand, as in photo A, by slightly bending the longer fingers to adjust to the shorter and tuck your thumb in. Your hand should resemble a spear.

To develop speed in the finger jab, you need a great deal of practice, and most of this will be the result of your own initiative. Speed relies on economy of motion, and the jab is one technique with which you have the opportunity to experiment. The jab, like all the JKD blows, must be thrust forward without any

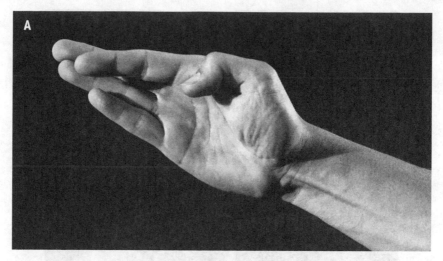

retracting motion. It is like a snake darting at its prey without warning.

The more hours you spend in speed hitting, the faster your hands will travel, as time goes by. Like the boxer who whips out his hands while jogging, you must also take solitary training seriously. One excellent training device for this is the paper target, as in photo B. It is so inexpensive and easy to construct and yet very valuable to anyone who wants to enhance his speed

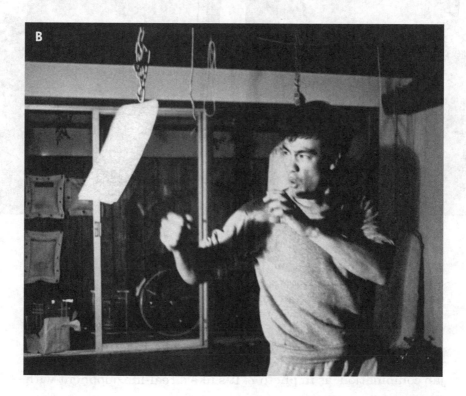

in punching or jabbing.

Besides the paper target, Lee used to practice on a thick leather strip to toughen his fingers, as in photo X. He also worked heavily on the bouncing head dummy, as in photo Y, which is excellent for finger jabbing. It gives when struck but is solid enough to harden the fingers.

Although the wooden dummy is too solid to jab your fingers into, it is a valuable apparatus with which to practice the finger jab combination, as in photo Z. It's like a real-life opponent with its arms outstretched and its leg impeding your approach.

The leading finger jab is the fastest hand weapon, and the leading straight is the fastest of all the punches. The leading straight is the backbone punch of jeet kune do. It is the main offensive weapon, but it is also an important defensive tool to stop and intercept a complex attack in an instant.

Although the leading straight punch has been discussed in Chapter 4, power is not one of its leading characteristics. Actually, the leading straight punch is more appropriately classified as a "speed punch." Like the finger jab, it travels only a short distance to the target, as in photos 1, 2 and 3, because

that hand is already extended and closer to its target.

Besides being the fastest punch, the straight lead is also the most accurate because it is delivered straightforward, at a close distance, and your balance is left intact. Like the finger jab, it is hard to block, especially if you keep it in a continuous, small motion. Besides, it can be delivered faster while in motion than from a fixed position. Like the finger jab, it keeps the opponent on edge by its threatening gesture.

Put some "zip" into your punch by snapping it just before impact. Keep your hand loose, and tighten your fist only an instant before contact. To put explosiveness in the blow, utilize the flowing-energy concept by adding heaviness to your hand.

The straight lead is not an end but a means to an end. It is not a powerful blow that will knock your opponent flat with one punch, but it is the most dominating punch in jeet kune do and is used profusely with the other combination punches and kicks.

The straight punch should be delivered from an on-guard position with the point of contact in line with the surface of your shoulder, as in photos 1, 2 and 3. Against a short opponent or if you are hitting at the low-line level, bend your knees so your shoulders are aligned to the point of contact. Likewise, if he is a tall person, stand on the balls of your feet.

Later, as you progress, the straight punch should be thrown from any position in which your hand happens to be, without any extra motion, like retracting it or pulling your shoulder back before delivery. But the punch must be launched with your body in balance to be effective.

Unlike the classical stance, the hand is never placed on your hip, as in photos A, B and C, nor is the punch initiated from there. It is impractical to have your hand traveling the extra, needless distance. Furthermore, delivery of your punch from the hip exposes a large area of your body during the action.

As discussed in the last chapter, the leading right will have more sting if you pivot your hips and utilize all the other functions for a heavy blow. But sometimes this will telegraph your movement, and you have to decide whether to sacrifice speed for power. This depends on your opponent. If he is very slow and awkward, you can utilize the powerful blows and still make contact. But if he is fast, you may have to concentrate on speed more than power. Among the best equipment to develop speed and accuracy in your punching is the old-fashioned speed bag, as in photo X (see page 96). The bag, supported by an elastic line to the ceiling and a rope to the floor, is suspended to your shoulder level. To use the bag properly, you have to be quick

with your hands. You have to hit the target perfectly so the bag will bounce directly back to you, and you need good timing with your hands.

In the beginning, use both hands to punch the bag and stand with your feet parallel but comfortably apart. Hit the bag directly straight, using your nose as the guiding point. The most valuable feature of the bag is that it compels you to hit directly and crisply and not push or it will not return to you sharply. But once you have the knack of punching it after several practices, you can then train in the on-guard position and employ the fist-and-elbow combination. Hit with your fist and block or strike

Z

with your elbow and forearm, as in photo Y.

You cannot hit the bag standing in the classical style, with your punch delivered from your hip, because it will be too late for you to react after the first punch. You are liable to be hit on your face because your hands will not be able to protect your head from the oncoming bag.

The punching pads, as shown in photo Z, are pieces of versatile equipment used to increase speed and heavy punching for kicking and applying combinations. You can work with one or two pieces.

In photos 1 and 2, Lee practices an explosive leading right punch with just one pad. Besides explosiveness, the one pad is good for developing speed in your punch. Have your partner hold out the pad. Whenever you attempt to punch, he jerks it swiftly either upward or downward, trying to make you miss when you attempt to hit it squarely.

In photos 1, 2 and 3, Lee throws his leading right and follows up with his left to the second pad. With a pair of pads, your partner can help you develop speed, aim and coordination by moving himself

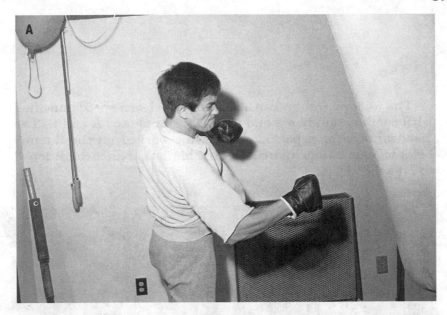

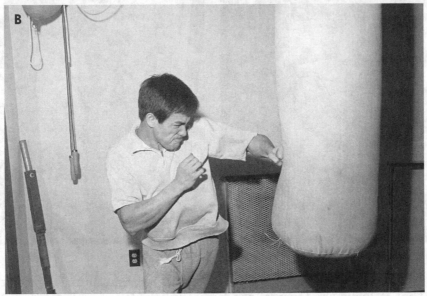

and his hands around—revealing a pair of elusive targets.

Punching the wall canvas bag is not recommended for speed. To develop speed, you must hit with speed in mind and not power. If you hit with full power all the time, you will be sacrificing speed. Even while hitting the heavy bag, as in photos A and B, you can hit with a combination of speed and power. Use your dominating, leading hand mostly for speed and your rear hand for power. From time to time, you can throw heavy punches from both hands as you "crowd" the bag.

The wooden dummy can also be used to learn speed punching with combination blows and parries, as in photos A and B. The disadvantage for a person who hasn't worked on the dummy before is that he can injure himself if his fists are not conditioned to hit solid objects.

The lead is almost like the leading straight punch, except that it lacks the force of the latter punch. It is used mostly as a "feeler" in the early rounds of sparring or in the beginning of a fight between two crafty fighters. The lead jab is used as a cautious measure to study the opponent in motion. When two evenly matched, skilled fighters meet, sometimes the lead jab is used throughout the fight.

The lead jab is generally the dominating hand technique in boxing, but in jeet kune do, it is the leading straight punch. Both techniques have almost the same features: speed, accuracy, short delivery, body balance in delivery, and both are hard to block.

In offense, the lead jab is used to keep the opponent off-balance and to create openings for more punishing blows. In defense, it is an effective maneuver to stop or meet an attack. For example, you can "beat your opponent to the punch" by throwing a quick jab to his face just as he is about to launch an attack. The jab can also be delivered from an extended arm to "stiff-arm" him, which keeps your opponent at a distance and prevents him from close-range fighting.

The jab is mostly focused on the face because it lacks force and does little damage to the body. It is a weaker, pestering strike, which is good as a stratagem to use against an opponent. It is also thrown with looseness in your arm and a snap before impact.

An excellent child's game that is fun and can be played with anyone is the "slapping" match. Extend your arm fully in front of you with your hand outstretched. Your thumb is on the top as you hold it vertically. When your partner swings his hand to slap yours, you react by jerking it suddenly upward and toward you, trying your best to avoid contact. You let him do the slapping until he misses, then you reverse roles.

Nontelegraphic Punch

One of the most distinctive features that sets jeet kune do apart from the classical styles of kung fu and boxing is that Bruce Lee incorporated the nontelegraphic aspects of fencing. By adopting part of its footwork and applying the principle of thrusting the hand before your body, it is almost impossible to parry or block the speed punches such as the backfist, jab or the lead punch.

The concept behind this is that if you initiate your punch without any forewarning, such as tensing your shoulders or moving your foot or body, the opponent will not have enough time to react. When he sees the punch coming—that is, if he ever sees it—it will be too late for him to block or parry it. Actually, the punch already makes contact, and your hand is snapping back when your body edges forward. It is the exact movement of the fencer who thrusts his foil forward and does not move forward until his hand is being retracted.

If you punch simultaneously, with just a slight motion of your feet or body, you have telegraphed or warned your opponent of your intention. The secret in the nontelegraphic move is to relax

your body and arms but keep them weaving in a slight motion. Whip out your hand loosely so your shoulders don't tense, and clench your hand just an instant before contact as you snap it. You have to keep a "poker face" while facing your opponent. A slight twitch or expression on your face may trigger your intention and warn your opponent.

Lee was so good in speed punching that he had a problem getting volunteers to come to him when he demonstrated in karate tournaments. Even the champions were afraid to confront him because most of them knew of his prowess with his hands. In photos 1 and 2, Lee demonstrated his speed against a karate black belt. Even after indicating to the volunteer where his punch would be directed, the black belt was unable to block his punch in eight tries. Lee was successful not just because of his quick hands but because of his flawless, nontelegraphic movement.

Use your nontelegraphic punch with your forward shuffle, as discussed in Chapter 3. Practice the backfist first, then the finger jab and finally the leading straight punch.

In the beginning, punch or jab into the air and subsequently on the paper target. Later, use the punching pad. Like training in speed punching, have your partner jerk the pad quickly when you throw your punch, trying his utmost to make you miss it.

Another exercise that you can include in your training is the "clapping" game. Stand about a full arm's length plus another four or five inches away from your partner. Let him keep his hands about a foot apart in front of him. The idea is to throw a punch to his face or body straight between his hands. It is a test as to whether you can hit the target and snap your fist before he can clap it between his hands.

If he can't, then let him reduce the distance between his hands until it is only about six inches. You can also step farther away from him while delivering your punch. But before you attempt to do this drill, be sure that you can control your punch. If he misses your blow, you should be able to stop your punch just above the surface of his skin.

It may be wise to learn control in punching first before you attempt the clapping exercise. Have your partner stand motionless; throw your punches about two inches from his face. Then gradually throw your punch closer and closer until you are barely touching his skin. Your partner should only feel the draft from your action. In the meantime, your partner can learn not to blink as the blow almost brushes his face.

A

Speed in Kicking

The most dominating JKD kicks are the side and hook kicks. The side kick can be used with quickness and power, while the hook kick is used mostly for speed. In jeet kune do, most of the kicks are launched from the leading foot, shortening the distance between yourself and the target.

The hook kick is focused generally on the upper line—from the waist to the head. It is especially effective when directed to the ribs of your opponent, just below his arm, as in photo A. As mentioned in the previous chapter, the leg is stronger than the hand so even a fast kick like the hook can disable your opponent with just one blow.

The hook kick is more difficult to learn than the side kick because it is harder to deliver and because it tends to throw you off-balance in the process, especially on the high kicks.

To do the hook kick, stand in the on-guard position, as in photo 1. Lift your lead knee until your thigh is horizontal, as in photo 2. Your lower leg (below the knee) should hang loosely and point to the floor at about a 45-degree angle. Your weight should be completely on the rear foot with the knee slightly bent and your body leaning backward. Then pivot on the ball of your rear foot, which automatically induces your hips to rotate. Finally, snap your foot from the knee, which straightens the supporting leg, as in photos 3 and 4. The hook kick is performed with just one motion from the time your foot leaves the floor. Your eyes should be constantly on the target and your kick is aimed not at the surface of the target but through it. Your foot, like the punch, should snap or whip just before impact.

PATH OF FOOT

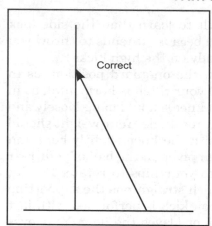

Correct

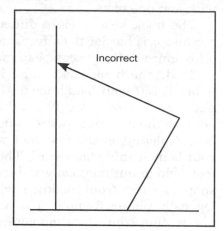

Incorrect

One fault of a beginner is that he leans too far forward and includes two motions in his hook kick. After raising his knee, he has a tendency to swing his foot back to deliver the kick. (See the chart on the path of your foot.) It slows down delivery, and the two motions weaken his blow because of the hesitation and the fact that he does not completely utilize the combined force of the hip and leg action, as Lee demonstrates in photos A, B, C and D.

The hook kick is usually quickly delivered with the quick advance footwork from the on-guard position, as in photo 1. Step forward about three inches, as in photo 2, then slide your rear foot quickly forward, as in photo 3. Just before your rear foot makes contact with the front one, lift your front foot to apply the kick, as in photo 4.

Sometimes, your opponent may "crowd" you and you may find yourself quite close to him. In this predicament, omit the three-inch step and, instead, from the on-guard position, as in photo 1, slide your rear foot quickly forward just behind the front foot, as in photo 2. Then, before your opponent can react, you should be

launching your hook kick, as in photo 3. This movement should be done with one fluid motion and with no hesitation or jerkiness in between.

Other times, you may find yourself caught at intervals. You may be too close to your opponent to take the three-inch step and too far to use the short slide, as in photo 2. When you are in that position, just do the forward burst or lunge, as in photo Y, before delivering the hook kick.

Although the hook kick is generally used for the upper-line attack, often it is aimed at the groin area, as in photos A and B. This depends on the angle of your body to your opponent's.

A

Many times you will learn that it is the only practical kick to reach the hard-to-hit areas.

There are several apparatuses you can train on to develop your hook kick. One of the most practical and least expensive is the paper target. From an on-guard position, kick the target at first without stepping out. Get the "feel" or balance of your stance and the path of your foot. Pay close attention to the snap at impact.

Gradually kick into harder objects such as the light bag, as in photo A, and the heavy bag. For combination hand and foot techniques, use the wooden dummy, as in photo B. Once you have acquired the knack of delivering the hook kick automatically, practice with a moving target such as the punching pad. In the beginning, just use one. Later, incorporate the other so you can drill both your left and right foot.

Although your instep is generally the point of contact in the hook kick, other regions of your foot can be used, such as the ball, toe or shin. But avoid using the toe or ball if you are sparring barefoot.

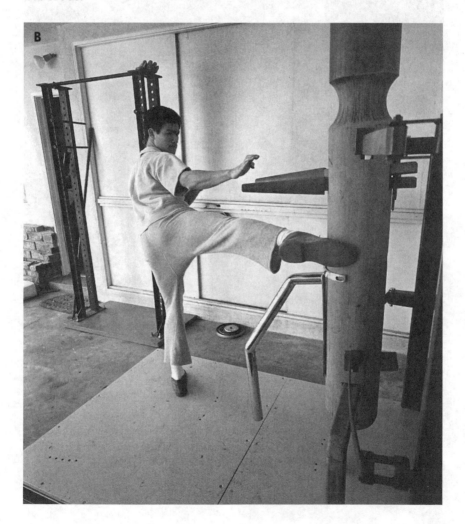

In most hitting, the powerful blows are usually slower than the lighter ones. But the side kick, which is the hardest blow you can release, is also a fast kick. If directed toward the low line such as the opponent's knee or shin, as in photos 1 and 2, it can be just as swift as the hook kick. Bruce Lee used to do his low-line side kicks almost as rapidly as throwing his leading jab. It was fascinating to see him chase his opponent, who was completely off-balance while reeling backward.

To develop a speed side kick, stand in the on-guard position and imagine that your opponent's leading leg is in front of you. Keep your eyes focused at your imaginary foe's face as you deliver a series of side kicks angling downward. The idea of this drill is to thrust your foot strongly but with speed and snap. The wooden dummy can also be used to practice the low side kick, as in photo A, or in combination with other hand or other foot techniques.

Another fast kick is the front or the upward groin kick. It is delivered almost exactly like the hook kick. Instead of the kick being

directed to the side of your opponent, so your foot travels obliquely, the kick is to the groin and travels straight upward or vertically. If used with your hip motion, as discussed in Chapter 4, you can generate a much more powerful blow than with the hook kick.

The front kick is not employed too often in JKD sparring because the on-guard stance doesn't allow too many opportunities for its use. But it is an effective weapon against many fighters who don't protect their groin area well.

Although the ball or toe of your foot can be the point of contact, predominantly the instep and shin are used. It can be delivered more accurately than with the toe or ball. Your foot will be traveling upward between your opponent's legs, as in photos 1 and 2. It is almost impossible to miss the target.

In sparring, infrequently you do have an opportunity to use the front kick. For example, after avoiding an attack, you may be able to swing your opponent around so his back faces you, as in photos A and B.

For your daily training, you can practice the front kick by hitting the bottom rim of a heavy bag. Other light bags or balls that can be suspended from the ceiling are excellent for practicing your skill against a moving object. The punching pad can be employed, too, by having your partner hold it horizontally with his palm facing the floor. Like the other techniques, the wooden dummy is used for combinations, as in photo Y, but you can't kick it too hard without risking injury to your foot.

Awareness

Some athletes seem to have greater peripheral vision than others, like a basketball player who seems to know where each player is and always seems to find the open man, or like a quarterback who always sees the unguarded receiver. Some experts in the sports field believe that the exceptionally high degree of peripheral vision possessed by a few athletes is innate. But they also believe that this trait can be broadened by everyone through constant practice.

In martial arts, you may not need as wide a range of vision as in other sports if you are confronted by a single person. But you surely need it when surrounded by two or more attackers.

To develop peripheral vision, focus your eyes at a distant structure, such as a high building or a pole. Then diffuse your sight so you can still see the structure clearly but also the blurry environment bordering it. Take note of any movements from both corners of your eyes.

In training, work with three or more people and spread them out. Your eyes seem to focus on the person in the middle, but your vision is actually on all of them. As one of them moves, no matter how slightly, call out his name.

Against one opponent, your eyes should be fixed on his eyes, but your vision should encompass his whole body, as in photo A. Your vision sphere is more extensive when focused at a distance,

and as you focus your sight closer, your sphere becomes smaller. Against an individual, it is harder to follow his hand motion—even though his hands are closer to your eyes than his feet—because hands move faster than feet.

One high-ranking martial artist was amazed at Bruce Lee's quick hand and foot reaction. Lee had the ability to kick just before his opponent kicked and punch just before his opponent punched. To those who saw him for the first time, he seemed to have an instinct or a sixth sense that let him read other people's minds. It could be frustrating to spar with someone like him because he was upon you before you could even blink your eye.

The secret of Lee's quick reaction was his highly developed sense of awareness, cultivated by years of training. It complemented his hand and foot techniques. Just the acceleration of your foot and hand doesn't necessarily mean that you will beat your opponent to the punch or kick. In other words, speed alone doesn't guarantee that your blow will reach your opponent before his reaches you. But by cultivating your keen sense of awareness, your chance of beating him is enhanced tremendously.

How does one develop his keen awareness? One way is to be alert to your surroundings. Learn to react quickly. For instance, while in a restaurant or other public place, select a person from the crowd and follow his movement. Whenever he or she gesticulates, you respond by a silent "ugh" or any other quiet, sharp sound. Gradually, increase your response by attempting to anticipate or beat his gesture with an "ugh."

If you have a dog, practice keen awareness by holding a rag before him. Whenever he jumps for it, react with an "ugh" as you simultaneously jerk the rag from his grasp. At the outset, hold the rag high, but as your reaction quickens, lower it toward him. You will be surprised how much this simple exercise can shorten your response time.

If you aren't convinced, do the same exercise without the sound and, instead, just jerk the rag away. You will then realize how slow your reaction can be.

An exercise that you can do with your partner is allowing him to gesticulate quickly as you react to him. Then later, hold the punching pad in front of him and let him hit it. As he throws his speed punch, jerk your hand quickly with a simultaneous "ugh." Incredibly, this simple exercise can add a great deal of speed to your punch and kick.

PART II
SKILL IN TECHNIQUES

Chapter 6
Skill in Movement

Skill In Movement

Skill in movement is very important in the art of fighting. It is heavily relied on in attack, defense, deception and conservation of energy. It is your proficiency in mobility or footwork that allows you to control the precise distance between you and your opponent. The strategy of footwork is to take advantage of your opponent's footwork with your own. Your attack or defense may be based on the opponent's foot pattern of advancing and backing off.

When you learn his foot pattern, adjust to it. You can then press (advance) or fall back (retreat) just enough to facilitate a hit. The length of your step is coordinated to your opponent's movement. Intuition in moving forward and backward is also an intuition of when to attack and when to defend.

A skilled fighter never stays in one spot long; he is in constant motion to baffle his opponent, causing him to misjudge the distance. A moving target is harder to hit, and by being in motion, you can move more quickly than from a set position.

By varying the distance and timing of your movement continuously, you can confuse your opponent. You will disturb his preparation to attack or defend, keeping him off-balance.

You must practice footwork with punching and kicking. Without footwork, the fighter is like an immobile cannon that cannot be directed at the enemy line. The speed and power of your punches and kicks depends on your nimble feet and balanced body.

A good fighter like Bruce Lee always seemed to do everything with ease, finesse and grace. He moved into his opponent, landed his blow without any effort and easily moved out of range. He always seemed to outhit and outguess his opponent. His timing was so good that he controlled even the opponent's rhythm. He moved with assurance and coordination.

A poor fighter, on the other hand, seems to move clumsily. He can't find the correct distance, telegraphs his intentions and never seems to outthink his opponent. Instead of controlling his opponent, he lets the opponent control him.

Distance

Distance continuously changes between two skilled fighters as both attempt to seek the most advantageous position. The best idea is to stay consistently out of range of the opponent's simple punch but not too far away to deliver an attack with just a short step forward. This distance is contingent not only on your own speed and agility but also that of your opponent.

In boxing, the fighters stand closer to each other than martial artists because martial artists utilize their feet to kick. The leg is longer than the arm, so the martial artist has a longer reach than a boxer.

In jeet kune do, there are three different distances in fighting. Generally, the longest range is employed when you don't know your opponent's prowess or his intention, as in photo 1, and you want to "feel" or "test" him out. In defense, it is wiser to stay too far away instead of too close to your opponent. But in a lengthy struggle, you are only safe at a distance if you can really outclass your opponent with speed and agility in movement.

Even if you are fast, it is difficult to parry a blow if you are too near your opponent. The one who initiates the attack usually has an advantage in close quarters. But an attacker who can't properly figure out distance will not succeed, even if he is accurate, quick, has good timing and utilizes economy of movement.

Once you think that you have the "feel" of your opponent, you move closer to him, to the medium distance, as in photo 2. From this distance, you can be just out of his range and yet close enough to launch an attack. It is a safe distance if you can also apply good timing. A skillful fighter will maneuver to entice his opponent to shorten the gap or distance until the opponent is too near to avoid the trap.

This medium distance also allows you to avoid any blow by a quick retreat or a backward burst. But to use this defensive strategy continuously is not always practical because it deprives you of a counterattack or delivery of your own offense. In jeet kune do, you retreat just far enough to evade the blow, but you stay just close enough for a counterattack.

Close-distance fighting usually is a consequence of an attack or a counterattack. It is harder to defend from this distance unless you have already trapped your opponent's arms. Definitely, the advantage is to the one who initiates the attack. At a close distance, as in photo 3, the fighter with the expertise of his hands will outwit the kicker.

However, a martial artist, unlike a boxer, needs to be alert to blows from the elbows, knees, head, etc., in close-range fighting. He also has to be aware of the chance of being thrown or grappled to the ground.

3

In boxing, the fighters have difficulty in closing in, and once they are there, it is more difficult for them to remain there. In martial arts, because the feet are employed, it is even more difficult to close in than in boxing. But once the fighters are in close proximity, the fight or match is over quickly because martial artists have too many offensive tactics to use.

In close-range fighting, it is imperative that you immobilize your opponent's lead foot by placing yours next to his, as in photo 3. This procedure should be done automatically because, at that close range, your concentration will be heavily focused on your hand techniques.

 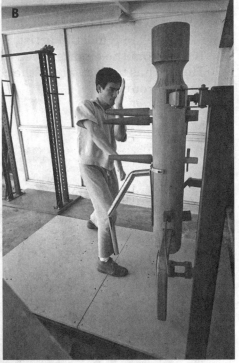

Lee constructed the metal bar on the wooden dummy to simulate his opponent's leg, as in photos A and B. At the outset, he had to concentrate heavily on the placement of his lead foot, but after a few months, it became a natural and habitual procedure.

An infighting maneuver that Lee used frequently was to keep his opponent off-balance by pressing him, as in photos Y and Z. This tactic can be used against anyone, even a heavier and stronger opponent. Practice this with your partner by bending your knees slightly, placing your weight on the front foot and shoving your partner vigorously without letting up. Your feet advance with a shuffle, and you use your hand and body to trap your partner's arms. The secret behind this force is to use your hips and not entirely your shoulders when you are pressing him.

Once you have your partner reeling backward, you can use your free hand to hit his body and then pin him to the ground. It is a safe maneuver because your partner cannot take the offensive. He is too off-balance to retaliate.

The better fighter is always maneuvering, trying to stay in the range that suits him best. He is just out of the opponent's attack range and patiently waits for the right moment to close in or draw the opponent toward him. He may attack as the opponent advances or when he sees an opening while the opponent is changing his pace or position.

The attack or retreat should be rapid, penetrating and spontaneous. The opponent should not be able to predict your movement until it is too late for him to retaliate or defend an attack. The ideal time for the attack to be delivered is when he is in a stupor.

Distance is so vital that even a small mistake in range can render an attack harmless. You should launch your attack just before the opponent is at your desired distance—not after he reaches the desired range. It is like in baseball when the outfielder begins to run in the right direction even before the batter swings the bat. Or it is like a football quarterback who throws the ball at the spot just before the receiver reaches it.

Footwork

Against a fighter who has a good sense of distance and is difficult to reach in frontal attacks, the maneuver to "bridge the gap," or to close the distance, is a series of steps backward while progressively shortening them. Or you can let your opponent take the initiative as he closes the distance when he lunges at you.

If you are against a defensive fighter with a good sense of distance, advance with a series of steps, making the first step smooth and economical. A clever maneuver is to advance a step or two and then retreat, enticing the opponent to pursue. If he does, allow him to take a step or two, then surprise him with a burst forward right into his track at the precise instant he raises his foot to step forward.

To confuse your opponent, vary the length of your steps and your speed, but use short steps when changing position. You can only refine your sense of distance by moving smoothly and quickly.

While sparring or fighting, use good footwork to be as near to your opponent as possible for retaliation. Move lightly with your knees slightly bent, always ready to spring forward when the opportunity arises.

Stepping forward with a feint adds speed to the attack and often creates openings as the opponent is forced to commit himself. Stepping back can be strategically used against an opponent who doesn't want to engage in close-quarter fighting or who stays too far away to be reached.

In photo 1, Lee remains at a far distance, cautiously waiting for the opponent to make his move. Just as his opponent launches his attack, as in photo 2, Lee quickly counters by moving in and clashing his leg against the opponent's lead leg, preventing him from delivering his high hook kick, as in photo 3. After stopping the attack, Lee takes the offensive by throwing a right punch, as in photo 4.

In order to beat his opponent to the blow, Lee needed quick reactions that came from his daily workouts, especially in developing his keen sense of awareness. You should also notice that he doesn't deliver his punch while his right foot is off the ground or when his body is not in alignment. His punch will make its contact as his body moves forward and his foot is just about planted.

You should always conceal your intention from your opponent. Sometimes, instead of countering by moving in, you do the

opposite by moving back. In photos 1 and 2, Lee moves back and calculates the opponent's timing and attack. He moves just far enough to ward off the penetrating side kick, as in photo 3, and still be in a good position to retaliate, as he does in photos 4 and 5, with a punishing punching attack.

In another illustration of the moving-back maneuver, the opponent fakes a punch to Lee's face, as in photos A and B. Lee reacts to the feint, as in photo C, but is fast enough to recover and move away from the real attack, as in photo D. He moves just enough to brush off the side kick and then counters—this time with a high hook kick to the opponent's face, as in photo E.

By retreating, you allow the opponent some room to kick, so it is a smart tactic sometimes to crowd or press him from launching his attack. A wise fighter generally strives to be an elusive and difficult target by not moving forward or backward in a straight direction from a medium distance.

In both counters, Lee has to lunge forward to reach the opponent and has to do it quickly before the opponent can recover to defend himself.

Side Stepping and Ducking

In jeet kune do, side stepping is a defensive science to avoid a punch or a kick. If done properly, it is a safe and valuable movement for counterattacking. The purpose of side stepping is not to avoid the opponent's onrush but his blow.

If the attack is shallow, the counter is quite simple. But if the attack is penetrating, such as a rush or deep lunge, it is not that easy. You have to move just enough to avoid the blow and be close enough to turn quickly and pounce on him just as he, or the blow, bypasses you.

In far-distance fighting, the defender usually has the advantage because he has enough time to prepare for the attack and has time to counter accordingly. In photo 1, Lee waits for his opponent to attack, and once the attack is on its way, he sidesteps to his left at the last moment, as in photos 2 and 3, barely avoiding the side kick. It is such a subtle movement that it does not "telegraph" or unbalance his body.

Once a kick or punch is committed, the attacker cannot deviate his blow from its path and expect to land it effectively. If the opponent is off his feet, as in photo 3, he has no way to alter his course.

In photo 4, the opponent lands just in front of Lee, perfect for a counterattack. In photos 5, 6 and 7, although Lee is in a good position to use a front kick to his opponent's groin, he throws a right punch and follows it up by dragging him to the floor.

Against an opponent's right lead punch, sidestep to the left by swaying your body and ducking your head toward the left without any loss of balance. As his punch passes over your head, pivot your body by throwing your hips into the opponent and simultaneously delivering a right to his body or jaw.

Ducking is dipping your body forward from the waist mostly to let the blow pass over your head. Its primary function is to

avoid blows and still be in range to counterattack.

This tactic must be employed with caution. If you duck from a feint or duck too early, you leave yourself wide open for a punch or a kick. Your only defense is to weave and quickly escape from that position. While ducking, keep your eyes constantly on your opponent and not on the floor. In photos A and B, Lee practices the tactic by swinging the heavy bag.

Most of your side stepping should be to the left against an unorthodox or right-lead fighter because, after he misses, he is

defenseless as you stand behind him. Sidestep to the right if he
is an orthodox fighter.

But in jeet kune do, sometimes you are compelled to sidestep
to the right to confuse the opponent. Sidestepping to the right
requires more skill in timing and in countering. Your timing and
movement must be better calculated than sidestepping to the
left. You also have to counter faster because the opponent still
faces you and is in position to deliver another attack.

In photos 1, 2 and 3, Lee avoids the side kick by sidestepping to his right. Notice that in photo 3, he uses his right hand to protect his body if he should ever misjudge the blow. In photos 4 and 5, Lee is in perfect position to deliver a kick to the groin area.

Frequently, your opponent's launched attack is so intense that he is not prepared to protect himself after a miss. Generally, he is vulnerable to an attack to the head and body. In photos A, B and C, the opponent lunges at Lee with a side kick. Lee quickly sidesteps to his right at the last moment to avoid the kick. Then he counters, as in photos D and E, by employing a high hook kick to the opponent's face.

Precision of movement is essential in your footwork. Especially in sidestepping to your right, you must move at the exact moment and let the blow just miss you. If you move too early, you will give the attacker time to change his tactic. It is better to move late than too early, but do not move too late and be hit.

Precision in movement means to move with balance. After avoiding the blow, you must always be prepared to defend against another attack or be prepared to counter. Precision can only be achieved by hours of training.

While shifting your feet to secure the proper distance, use broken rhythm to confuse your opponent as to your distance. Be in the on-guard position to move quickly and easily.

When practicing offensive and defensive skills, you should always practice by combining footwork with them. No matter how simple the hand or foot techniques are, you should synchronize them while advancing and retreating. Eventually this type of training will develop your natural perception of distance and ability to move gracefully.

CHAPTER 9

Chapter 7
Skill in Hand Techniques

Skill in Hand Techniques

Skill in punching doesn't mean only delivering a strike and hitting your target. Accuracy, speed and powerful punches are also part of the technique of punching. Other elements include the position of your body when the punch is delivered, the path of your punch moving forward as well as returning, and the way your punch is thrown.

The most used and the most important punch in jeet kune do is the leading straight punch. It is a fast punch because it travels only a short distance; it is an accurate punch because it goes straight forward. It is also thrown with a minimum effort and consequently does not disturb your balance.

JKD vs. Classical

The leading straight punch is launched from an on-guard position, and the trajectory of your punch should be a straight line in front of your nose, as in photos 1, 2 and 3—using your nose as the guiding point.

One of the big advantages of the JKD delivery is that you can throw a leading straight punch and still be well covered. Your body is protected, and you are also in position to recover quickly from a miss.

In comparison, the classical system initiates a punch from the hip and exposes that section to an attack, as in photos A, B and C. When the punch is completed, it ends at one side of the body and the other portion of the body, especially the face, is exposed when the hand is withdrawn to the hip, as in photo C.

In photos 1 to 4, you will notice the difference in delivery between the classical system (left) and the JKD system (right). In the JKD system, as in photo 1, the hands protect the face and both the right and left sections of the body evenly, while in the classical system, only the left side of the body is protected. In photos 2 and 3, the JKD fighter has already delivered his punch completely, while the classical fighter is still in the process. Photo 4 shows where the blow ends in both systems.

In photo A, Lee (right) demonstrates from the on-guard position the short distance his punch has to travel compared to the classical stylist's. Apparently, this is also why his punch reaches the target much more quickly.

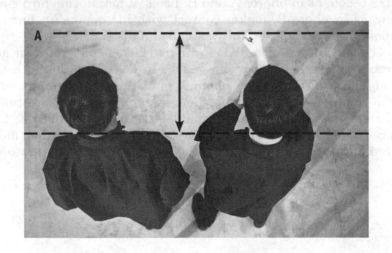

1

Throwing your punch with your fist kept vertically instead of horizontally like the classical system, as in photo 1, affords you extra reach, as in photos A and B. Lee's punch in this bird's-eye view, as in photo B, makes contact with his opponent, but the opponent's punch, even fully extended, falls short.

The advantage of a JKD straight lead is that you can add three or more inches to your reach. In jeet kune do, both the straight short lead, as in photo X, and the long straight lead, as in photo Y, are used. The short is employed for close-range fighting and the long for the middle distance. In photo X, Lee places his left hand on his right arm to indicate how much more extension he can administer in the long straight, as in photo Y.

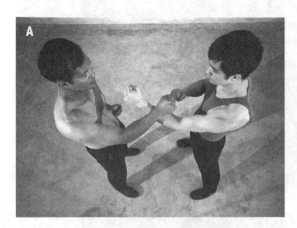

The rear or guarding hand should always be held high to protect your upper body from a counterattack. The rear hand does most of the guarding and is a supplement to the other hand. If one hand is punching, the other should be returning to protect the body or immobilizing the opponent's arm or arms against countering. It should always be there, correlating to the uncovered line or unprotected area. And it should also be in a tactical position for a follow-up.

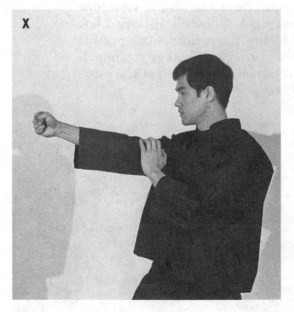

Punching Straight

In photos 1 to 5, Lee demonstrates from a bird's-eye view how he throws a combination of a lead right, follows it up with a left and finishes it off with a right. Notice the synchronizing of his hands as well as the protection they provide. Whether you punch with your lead or rear hand, your punch should land at the same spot, using your nose as the guiding point.

Punching straight before your nose and keeping your rear hand up is definitely superior to the classical system, as illustrated by Lee in photos A to C. As the lead hand is thrust forward, the rear hand is always ready to block or parry any blow to the body. It is also ready to counter. In photo A, the punch is partially blocked, but this doesn't stop it from penetrating and hitting the opponent's face.

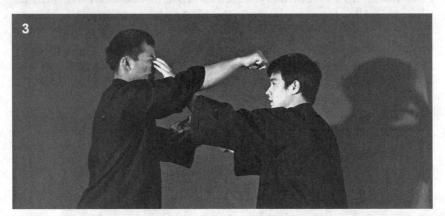

In this second illustration, as in photos 1, 2 and 3, when Lee's lead punch is blocked, he throws a straight jab directly in front of his nose, which wards off the opponent's punch as it proceeds straight toward his opponent's eye. Keeping the "centerline" thrust has a great advantage when two punches are thrown in the same path simultaneously against each other.

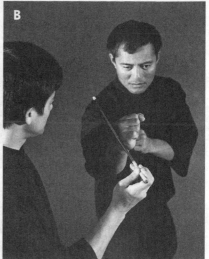

The position of your lead hand should allow you easy delivery and at the same time maximum security. In photos A and B, the hand is placed to deflect the blows to the side, and in photo Y, the punch is diverted downward with the defender hardly altering his hand.

As you have learned in chi sao, your elbow must maintain sturdiness, otherwise your defense may wither. Your elbow can move from side to side but must not collapse toward your body from a blow. After shooting out a punch, do not drop your hand when withdrawing it to the on-guard position. The punch should always be returned on the same plane or path it was delivered, as in photos 1, 2 and 3, so you are ready for any counter.

Bad Habits

Although you often see a good fighter with a bad habit, he usually gets away with it because of his superior speed and his good judgment in timing and distance. In photos A, B and C, Lee snaps back from a straight punch and counters with his left as the opponent creates an opening for Lee when he drops his hand in the withdrawal.

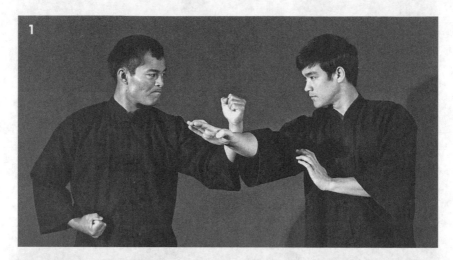

In another illustration, Lee converts a block by his opponent into a backfist punch when the opponent retracts his hand to throw another punch, as in photos 1, 2 and 3. If the opponent uses his left hand to immobilize Lee's right hand, as in photo 1, and throws a body punch with the other hand, he can keep Lee on the defensive. But the classical way of withdrawing his hand to his hip has given Lee the chance to convert a block into an offensive weapon, as in photo 2. The opponent's second punch is easily stopped by Lee's rear hand, as in photo 3.

Another bad habit some fighters develop is dropping their rear hand in the middle of exchanging blows, as in photos X and Y. In photo X, Lee takes advantage of such an opponent by slipping a punch and countering with a finger jab to his throat.

You can also take advantage of an opponent who lacks quick decision. He intends to throw his lead punch but after extending it halfway, he withdraws his hand to the on-guard position. During his indecisive moment, you can take advantage of his action by shooting a straight thrust, especially if he has already taken a step forward.

Then there is the fighter who continually engages and then disengages haphazardly. He will engage or make contact with your hand and, instead of keeping it there, lower or drift it to the opposite line, creating an opening for a quick, straight thrust.

In heavy punching, your arm becomes a weapon with your wrist, making it one solid piece like a club. The forearm is the handle and the fist is the knot, as in photo A. The fist is aligned with the forearm and does not bend at the wrist. At the completion of the punch, your clenched thumb should be up. Your fist propels without a twist, and the knuckles point at the direction of your body movement.

When punching with the lead hand, constantly vary the position of your head to protect it from a counter. Keep your opponent guessing. In your forward movement, your head remains straight during the first few inches, but later your head alters according to the situation.

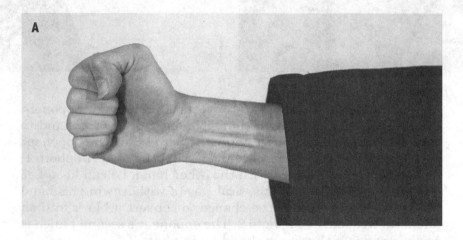

A

Another tactic is to feint before leading to lessen any countering blow. But keep everything simple; do not overplay the feinting or head motion. Frequently, you can surprise your opponent with a double-lead because the second punch may disrupt his timing and lead the way for a follow-up.

Sometimes a fighter attempts to put too much weight or "body" into his punch, and consequently, the blow becomes a push-punch, which lacks a powerful impact force. To be effective, the punch should always be delivered with your arms and shoulders loose. Your fist only tightens immediately before impact. Punches should never be thrown from a windup motion.

Some fighters have a good stance, but as soon as they are ready to attack, they leave themselves wide open, as in photo Y. They

develop this bad habit with a bad training attitude, as in photo Z. When practicing with the heavy bag, always maintain good form, as in photo 1. Have your partner pay close attention to your faults.

Some martial artists practice their art in slow motion. They move their hands and feet as slow as a snail. But they claim that when the time comes, they can ward off any attack quickly and effectively, even without speed training.

Lee used to emphasize that to be fast you have to practice fast movements. "I don't know any sprinter in the world who can break the record only by jogging daily around the track," he said.

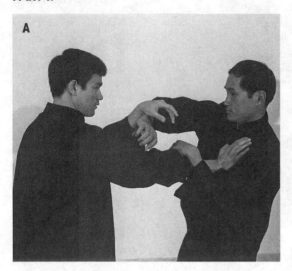

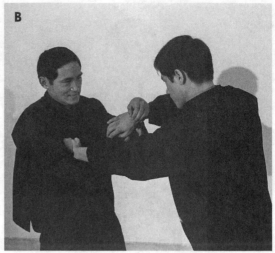

Trapping and Grabbing

Muscles do not act by themselves without guidance. It is the nervous system that guides them to perform. A well-executed movement is the consequence of daily training for skill by developing proper coordination of the nervous system with the muscles. These muscles contract at the exact fraction of a second with the precise degree of intensity or looseness, depending on the command of the nervous system.

The coordination or connection between the nervous system and the muscles improves with each performance. Each effort not only strengthens the skill but also paves the way for the succeeding acts to become easier, more definite and more exact. But absence from performance deteriorates the connection and affects the execution of the movement.

From the chi sao (sticking hands) exercise, as in photos A and B, the practitioners of wing chun advance to trapping hand (phon sao) or grabbing hand (lop sao) techniques. In photo 1, as Lee rotates his hand routinely in chi sao, he feels his partner's energy being disrupted and flowing sporadically. At that instant when there is a gap, Lee makes his move by overlapping his left hand over both of the partner's hands, as in photo 2. Then, as soon as he immobilizes or traps (phon sao) them, he throws a straight punch to his partner's face, as in photo 3.

The chi sao exercise is an important part of jeet kune do borrowed from wing chun kung fu. First, it develops sensitivity and pliability in your hands, which are so valuable in close hand-to-hand combat. You can really frustrate your opponent—who doesn't have that skill—because every move can be easily thwarted once you have developed this sensitivity. For more discussion on chi sao, go to pages 38 and 70.

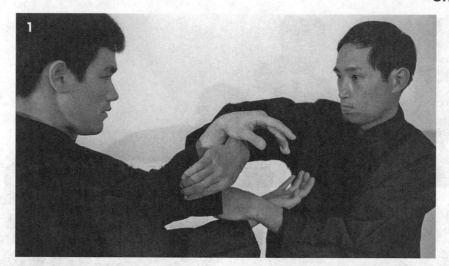

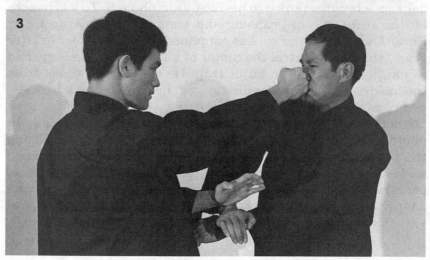

In photos 1, 2 and 3, Lee demonstrates the technique of grabbing (lop sao) from the chi sao exercise. In photo 1, Lee purposely exaggerates his rotation to narrow the space between his hands. When his hands are at the nearest position to each other, he grabs his partner's left arm with his left hand. During that instant, his arms cross each other, as in photo 2. Then Lee jerks his partner's arm toward himself and simultaneously delivers a backfist punch to his face, as in photo 3. To learn more on the technique of grabbing and trapping, read *Wing Chun Kung-Fu* by J. Yimm Lee. Lee simplified his chi sao a lot in later years. He would control the center of his opponent's energy and would not disengage to hit or trap. He would just attack from the inside. If his opponent disengaged, he would attack inside.

From close-quarters fighting, students are taught to move farther apart and continue to apply the hand techniques. In photos A, B and C, Lee's opponent attempts a finger jab utilizing the "centerline" thrust. He first attempts to push Lee's hand aside to create an opening, as in photo A. Second, he tries to penetrate Lee's defense with a finger jab, but Lee's flowing energy is too powerful to oppose, as in photo B. In photo C, the situation completely turns around as Lee takes the offensive.

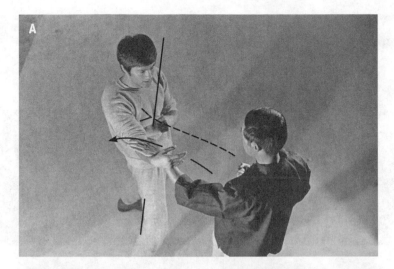

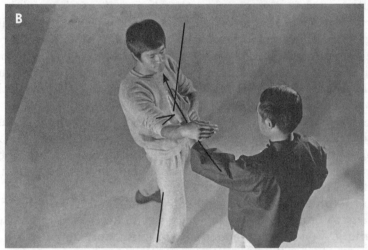

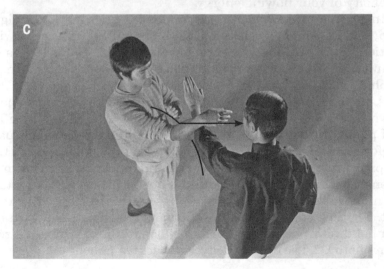

Y

Although Lee always takes the stance of jeet kune do's on-guard position, as in photo Y, he purposely stands in the modified wing chun stance, as in photo A, for the sake of illustrating the evolution of wing chun techniques in jeet kune do. With his body leaning a little backward, he sinks his hips toward the floor. Unlike a wing chun stylist, who faces his opponent squarely, Lee adopts the right lead stance.

As the opponent drives his lead punch toward his face, as in photo B, Lee, with quick reaction and anticipation, retaliates with a finger jab. By utilizing the centerline principle, Lee's thrust penetrates straight to the opponent's eye and simultaneously wards off his blow, as in photo C.

In the previous technique, Lee's opponent fails to deliver the inner-gate punch but Lee is successful. The reason is that this technique is not only dependent on execution but also on the intensity of your flowing energy.

In photos A, A1 and A2, the opponent engages Lee's right lead, but Lee quickly releases it with a small, counterclockwise motion, as in photo A1. Then he pivots his hips to his left as he simultaneously throws a right punch into his opponent's face, as in photo A2.

Against an opponent who hits and attempts to press his guard down, Lee uses the roll-and-trap maneuver, as in photos D to D2 and photos D to F (see page 160). In photo E, the opponent uses his forearm to hit and press Lee's right lead hand downward. Lee keeps his rear hand high for security and quickly rolls his arm to disengage, as in photo F. He continues to flow his energy and retain the immovable elbow position as he switches his weight to the front foot. Then he quickly traps the opponent's leading hand with his rear hand, as in photo D1. Once the opponent's hand is immobilized, as in photo D2, Lee quickly delivers a backfist punch.

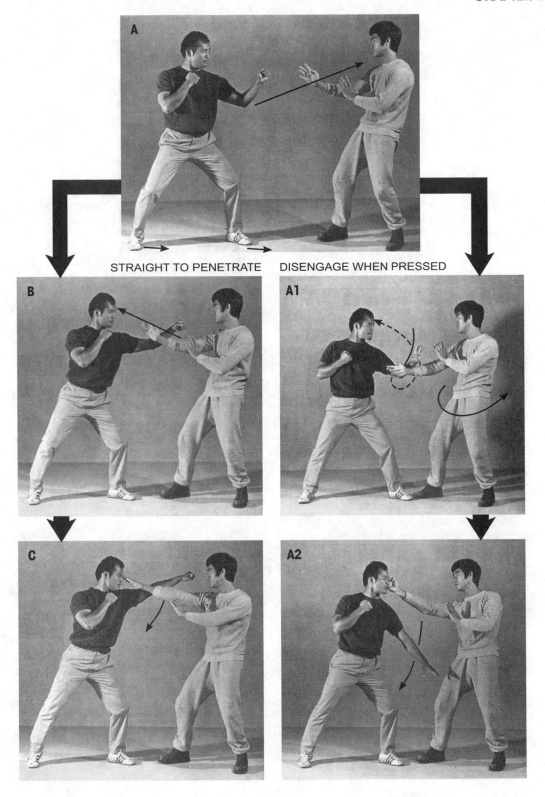

STRAIGHT TO PENETRATE   DISENGAGE WHEN PRESSED

ROLL TO DEFLECT   TRAP TO IMMOBILIZE

RECEIVE TO DETAIN   PURSUE WHEN WITHDRAWN

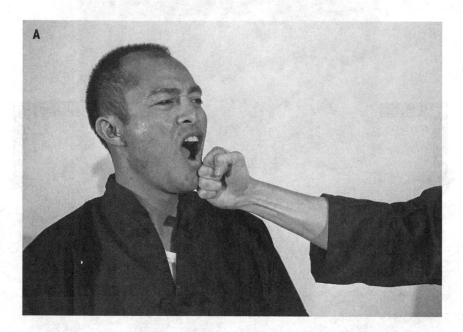

In photos G to G2 and G to I (see page 161), Lee illustrates a defensive maneuver of receiving a blow and then pursuing or countering it when the hand is being withdrawn. For instance, when the opponent delivers a punch to his body, Lee steps back slightly and rides the opponent's punch with his lead hand, preventing him from penetrating, as in photos H and I.

When the opponent withdraws his hand to throw another punch, as in photo G1, Lee quickly counters with a jab, as in photo G2, using his rear hand to stop the second punch.

Blinking is a natural response when an object is hurled toward your eyes. But in sparring or fighting, this reaction must be controlled or it will affect your defense as well as your counterattack. The instant your eyes are closed, you cannot react quickly enough to counter because you may not know where your elusive opponent is. Second, your adversary can take advantage of your shortcoming by feinting an attack. He can fake a punch, and as you blink, he can launch his blow while your eyes are shut.

While training in any type of fighting, it is important that you do not develop bad habits that may cause injury to yourself.

One of the most common faults of a beginner is that he has a tendency to open his mouth while in the midst of exchanging blows. It may be a habit he has acquired before studying martial arts, or he may have to breathe through his mouth because he is out of shape.

When your mouth is open, it can easily be broken by a direct hit, as in photo A. Another dangerous trait is to stick your tongue out, as in photo B. Learn to close your mouth in sparring or fighting by clenching your teeth firmly together. In sparring sessions, bite on your rubber mouthpiece to prevent it from flying out, even after a hard hit.

Protect your hands and wrists by punching correctly. Punch with your fist by having your fingers tightly clenched and your thumb wrapped snugly over them so you can't break it. Because the knuckles are the hardest part of your fist, this is the area that should make the contact, not your fingers.

Prevent any chance of spraining your wrist by keeping it aligned and firm when punching. Learn to hit straight by practicing on a makiwara (padded striking post), canvas bag or heavy bag.

Chapter 8
Skill in Kicking

Skill in Kicking

Although the hands are considered the most important tools, the feet can be a vital and integral part in your overall strategy in fighting. For instance, against a clever boxer, it is an advantage for you to use your feet all or most of the time. A boxer, who doesn't know any defense against a kick, is vulnerable, especially at the low-line area around the groin and knee.

The strategy is to use your feet and stay away from his fists. This is possible because the leg is longer than the arm. Besides, a proper delivery of a kick is usually more powerful than a punch.

In jeet kune do, the first line of attack or defense is the side kick to the shin or knee because those targets are closest to you and because they are exposed and difficult to protect. Furthermore, you are at a secure distance in delivering the kick, which can cripple your adversary with one blow. Bruce Lee used to apply this low kick like a jab. His kick was so quick that he could deliver multiple blows in a second.

To do the low side kick from an on-guard position, as in photo 1, slide your right or lead foot forward about three or four inches while you immediately bring your rear foot forward, just behind the lead foot. Then simultaneously lift your lead foot, as in photo 2, and deliver a low side kick by thrusting your foot obliquely and twisting your hips strongly, as in photos 3 and 4. Learn to keep your body away from your opponent's reach by leaning away from him and not upright, as in photo A.

Leading Side Kick to High Kick

The leading side kick is the most powerful kick in jeet kune do. One good kick is usually sufficient to knock your opponent off his feet. Although this is one of the most popular kicks, it should be employed with caution because it can be blocked or your leg can be seized if the kick is not delivered properly and at the right moment. But because of its tremendous force, sometimes it will penetrate a block, or the block is not effective enough to keep the blow from scoring or maiming. The side kick is not fast or as deceiving as some of the other kicks, but it can be used cleverly when preceded by a feint. A good feint with your hands should open the defense for a quick side kick to the head or body.

The leading side kick can be used in a defensive tactic, too. For instance, as your opponent makes his move to attack, you "cut-off" or "stop-kick," intercepting his movement with a quick side kick to his body before his blow reaches you.

The best equipment on which to practice your side kick is the

heavy 70-pound bag, as in photos A and B. The bag is durable enough to take any punishing blow and is heavy enough to give you a feeling of hitting a person. When contact is made, it emits a sound to let you know whether the contact was solid or "pushy."

Sometimes it is a good idea just to keep side-kicking the heavy bag as it sways back and forth. After a solid kick, wait for the bag to swing back, then time yourself with a leap and another side kick. Keep doing this for a good workout with your feet. Be careful that you don't miss the bag or fail to hit it squarely because you are liable to hurt your knee after a strong thrust.

Another good drill is having someone stand behind the bag. After a solid side kick, instruct him to move a step back and hold the bag in a slanting position so you can deliver another kick without stopping your motion. To do the second kick, you must plant your foot down immediately after the initial kick and deliver another side kick without the three-inch slide. In other words, the second kick is like the first without the slide.

To do the high or medium-level side kick, stand at the on-

guard position. Slide your lead foot three or four inches, as in photo 1. Then do the quick advance or the forward burst, as in photo 2, depending on the space between you and the opponent. Just when your rear foot is being planted, your lead foot should be delivering the kick, as in photos 3 and 4. The power in the kick comes from the sudden twist of the hips before impact and from the snapping of your foot after kicking through.

The side kick must be delivered with one fluid motion, as in

photos A to D. From an on-guard position, Lee fakes a punch to the opponent's face, as in photos A and B, luring the opponent to raise his hands, which leaves a gap in his midsection area. Then Lee quickly follows up with a side kick, as in photos C and D.

Other important apparatuses, which Bruce Lee utilized constantly, are the heavy shield and the air bag. The air bag is good as a stationary target, but the heavy shield is good for both stationary and moving targets.

Although the heavy shield cannot cushion the shock of the impact to the holder like the air bag, the holder can nullify some of the shock by moving backward. Because the heavy shield allows mobility on the part of the holder, the kicker can unleash his most powerful kick without hurting the other person.

In photo 1, Lee prepares to attack from the on-guard position. The holder of the heavy shield begins to move backward as he sees the attack unfolding, as in photo 2. But he is not quick enough and Lee releases a side kick, as in photos 3 and 4. The kick almost drives the holder off his feet, as in photo 5. This type of training develops a sense of distance and improves the timing of both individuals. The air bag is not appropriate as a moving target because of its limited hitting space.

To kick high, have someone hold a long staff at your waist level. Stand about five feet away and raise your right foot as high as possible with your leg bent and slanted. This can be accomplished by lifting your knee as high as possible. Lean your body backward so your head inclines toward your right. Then skip on your left foot toward the staff until your right foot passes over it.

The purpose of this training is not to kick but to learn to lift your foot as high as possible. Keep increasing the height of the staff until your foot can't pass over it anymore. Then do the same exercise, minus the staff, and kick into the air. To kick much higher, for instance, like over your head, you have to concentrate heavily on flexibility exercises.

In your daily practice, include the "rapid-fire" side-kick drill. Stand with your feet parallel, place your weight on your left foot, lean backward and execute a right side kick to your right. Then quickly position your right foot at the same spot after snapping it out. But just before you plant it, your left foot should be in motion for a left side kick to your left. As your left foot is being retrieved, immediately do another right side kick and keep repeating the kicks from one foot to the other as fast as you can. At the outset, you will feel awkward and off-balance, but continue to practice this difficult exercise daily for several minutes until you can do it fluently and in balance.

Hook Kick

One of the most utilized kicks in jeet kune do is the hook kick. It is not a powerful kick, but it is swift and deceptive. It is not a forceful kick, but it can be damaging. The big advantage the hook kick has over the side kick is that it can be launched in many instances before your opponent can prepare for it. It is also a safer kick because you can recover quickly after delivery. It is employed at a closer distance than the side kick but employed at a farther distance in the hand-to-hand fighting range.

To do the hook kick, slide your lead foot three or four inches forward from the on-guard position, as in photo 1. Then do the forward shuffle or the quick advance. As soon as your rear foot is about to land, deliver your side kick, as in photo 2. The kick should be concluded with a snap and your body should be leaning back, as in photos 3 and 4, and not forward.

Although the hook kick is used mostly for the upper line—above the waist—sometimes it can be used to attack the thigh or groin area, as in photo A. But this depends on the position of your opponent in relation to yours. He should be standing extremely to your right if you're in a right stance to hit his groin area. The hook kick to the thigh area is hardly ever used because it isn't too effective. The distance your foot has to travel is too short to generate enough power.

Spin Kick

The spin kick is used mostly as a counterattacking maneuver. It is very effective against an aggressive opponent who keeps attacking in a straight line but is not lunging at you. It is dangerous to use the spin kick against a defensive or counterattacking opponent who constantly waits for your move before retaliating. Against such an opponent, you are vulnerable just before you can shoot out your kick, when your back is turned to him.

The spin kick is a little more difficult to execute because you must rotate your body, and in the process, your back will be facing the target for an instant. At that point, you can easily misjudge the position of the target. Frankly, it takes several hours of practice before you can even hit the target squarely.

The spin kick is not a sweeping kick, as used by some martial artists, but similar to a back thrust kick. This is one of the few kick techniques in jeet kune do that employs the rear foot.

The best equipment for practicing the spin kick is the heavy

bag. Stand about a leg-length from the bag in the on-guard position, as in photo 1. Concentrate on the spot on the bag you wish to hit so that, while your body is rotating like a swivel, as in photo 2, you can still picture the spot in your mind.

The pivot should be done on the ball of your right foot with your head slightly ahead of your lower body so you have a glimpse of the target before you thrust your foot out, as in photo 3. Your body should be aligned with the bag when you deliver the kick. Like the side kick, you should "whip" your hips in at the time of contact and snap your foot, as in photo 4. It is very difficult to maintain your balance after the kick because your body is rotating and because you must thrust your foot at the same time.

The spin kick is a surprise countering tactic. Even against a veteran fighter who has good defense, the spin kick is often the only kick that can catch him off his guard. Because it takes so much practice to perfect this kick, learn to kick into the air as often as you can.

In the beginning, learn to do the technique slowly by standing in the on-guard position, as in photo 1. Then rotate your body on the ball of your slightly bent foot, as in photo 2. Keep your other leg bent and ready to thrust. Be sure that the lifted foot does not swing haphazardly in the pivot or it will throw you off-balance. Besides, you can't kick effectively with an outstretched foot. Finally, thrust your foot with force when your body has made almost a complete 180-degree rotation, as in photos 3 and 3A.

Other Kicks

The sweep or the reverse hook kick is not often used in jeet kune do because it lacks power. It is used strictly as a high kick to the face. The kick is employed mostly as a surprise tactic, especially against someone who attacks with his leading foot extended. A front or hook kick will not work because the path of your foot will be hampered by the extended foot. But a sweep will work easily because it will avoid the obstructive foot.

To do the sweep kick, you have to have flexible legs. From

3A

the on-guard position, as in photo 1, slide your lead foot about three or four inches forward and then do the quick advance as you initiate your kick, as in photo 2. If you are in the right lead stance, your foot will travel from your left to your right (clockwise motion) in a narrow arc, as in photos 3 and 3A.

This kick is a scraping-type of kick and will not knock your opponent down. If done with your shoes on, it can cause damage by scratching your opponent's face.

To practice this kick on a heavy bag from a right lead position, stand slightly toward your left and hit the bag with one motion. The path of the foot should be almost vertical, except for a small arc at the peak. The point of contact is the heel and outside blade of your right foot.

The latest kick that Bruce Lee developed for jeet kune do was the inside kick. This kick is applied at the low line, especially to the groin and inside thigh areas. The point of contact is your instep.

The kick, which is as fast as the front and hook kicks, is used against someone whose stance is the opposite of yours. For instance, if you are in the right lead stance and your opponent is in the left lead stance, you cannot hit his groin area with most kicks because his left leg protects it. But an inside kick—which is delivered like a front kick, except that it is not delivered vertically—can reach that area if you are standing slightly toward your left, angular to your opponent.

Unlike a front kick, the inside kick is delivered in an upward slant, opposite of the hook kick. But like the front kick, power can be created by jerking your hips forward just before contact. It is a difficult kick with which to generate power because you must have perfect synchronization between your hips and delivery of the kick.

The only other kick that is sometimes used is the front kick, which was discussed in Chapters 4 and 5.

3A

Chapter 9
Parrying

Parrying

Parrying is a defensive tactic that can easily be learned and applied. It is a quick motion with your closed or open hand, either from the inside or the outside, to ward off blows directed at you. It is just a light slap to the opponent's hand with hardly any force—just enough to deflect the blow away from your body.

The technique should be done with your elbow almost at a fixed position while the movement comes from your hand and arm. It should not be an extreme reaction such as a slashing or whipping motion. Any excessive movement of your hand will expose your body to a counterattack. In other words, you should move your hand just enough to protect and control the blow.

Timing in this technique is more important than force. If you react too early, your opponent can either change the path of his kick or punch. Or you may leave openings for a counter by parrying late, waiting until the last moment, and only acting when the blow is near you.

Against a quick, penetrating opponent or against someone with superior height and reach, you may have to take a step backward while parrying. The parry should be made simultaneously with your back foot in motion and not after it is planted, nor should the parry be made prior to your body movement.

Learn to parry only against a real attack. But if you intuitively start to parry against a feint or false attack, your motion should be controlled so that your hand or arm hardly reacts.

Train yourself to detect a real and false attack by having someone direct various kicks and punches at you. After a considerable amount of practice, you will only parry at the real attacks and not react to the feints or fakes.

Generally, a parry is a good and safe defensive measure, but a skilled fighter may beat your parry. If he does, then you must move backward while parrying.

Inside High Parry

The inside high parry is generally utilized because most attacks are punches directed to the face. In comparing the classical style with jeet kune do, as in photo A, it is discernible that the JKD way of parrying provides more protection and more speed on the upper line. In photo B, it reveals that a punch can be delivered almost simultaneously with the parry in jeet kune

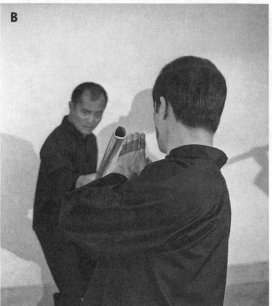

do. But this is not true with the other style, which uses a block and a punch; it is definitely a slower counter because of its two distinct motions.

Bruce Lee uses a long staff to practice the inside high parry, as in photos A and B. A partner thrusts the staff directly to Lee's face. Lee slips the thrust by shifting his weight to the lead foot and bending the front knee slightly. At the same time, he uses his left hand to parry the staff lightly. This type of training is valuable because your partner can spot any discrepancy in your balance and motion. Against any heavy blow such as a kick, use your parry with a clenched fist, as in photo C.

To defend against a swing, Lee, standing in the on-guard position, as in photo 1, prepares for the attack. As soon as his opponent initiates his swing, Lee already has his right hand in motion, as in photo 2. By the time he parries the punch, Lee's right punch is upon the opponent's face, as in photo 3. In photo Z, he uses the same parry against a straight right punch.

The inside high parry is done with a slight, counterclockwise twist of your wrist, as your hand meets the blow. This slight motion is capable of protecting your body because the twist of your wrist is away from your body and toward the oncoming blow. Your arm is stronger when it is directed away from your body rather than toward it. The classical style uses the opposite motion. The twist is clockwise toward the body.

Inside Low Parry

The inside low parry is used against a punch or kick in the low-line area. From a right-lead on-guard position, the parry is

made with a semicircular, clockwise, downward motion, as in photo 1. Simultaneously, your weight is shifted to the front leg as you bend your knee slightly. Almost at the same time, you counter with your right hand, as in photo 2.

In the classical system, your blocking hand moves downward in an oblique direction, as in photo A, as your other hand retracts toward your hip, as in photo B. The disadvantage in the classical style is that your countering is much slower because you have to block, while retracting your other hand, and then deliver your punch; these are two definite motions while there is just one fluid motion of both hands in jeet kune do. Another disadvantage is that your body, especially the upper line, is continuously exposed.

In the above photos, Lee illustrates the application of the inside low parry. In photo 1, Lee stands in the on-guard position, keeping his eyes glued on the opponent. As soon as the opponent begins to attack, Lee already responds to his action, as in photo 2.

The opponent throws a right that is intercepted by Lee's inside low parry, as in photo 3. Lee then converts the parry to a lop sao or grabbing technique. In one almost smooth motion, he pulls his opponent toward him and shifts his body forward to deliver a straight lead to the face.

Outside High Parry

The outside high parry is more of a slapping stroke than the inside high parry, which is more of a warding-off motion. This parry is used to divert the blow on the opposite side of your body, so your hand has to cross over, as in photo A. There is no loss in the counterpunch's quickness because your lead hand can still deliver the punch almost at the same time as you are parrying. By utilizing the guard or rear hand for parrying, the lead hand, which is closer to your opponent and is the stronger hand, is free to punch, as in photo B.

The classical system uses the same block for both the outside and inside high attack by just reversing the function of the hands. Instead of the left doing the block, the right does the blocking, and the left or the weaker hand does the punching, as in photo Y.

Bruce Lee explains in the following series of photos how he utilizes his outside high parry for defense against a "head" shot. In photo 1, Lee waits for his opponent's first move. In photo 2, as the opponent throws a right, Lee parries the blow with a light slap—just enough to divert the path of the blow from his face. Simultaneously, he takes a three or four inch slide forward with his lead foot, bending his knee so the weight is placed on it.

Trapping the opponent's parried hand, he delivers his own right, as in photos 3 and 3A (side view). If Lee were to block or slap the blow vigorously, he would not be able to trap the opponent's hand to his shoulder.

SIDE VIEW

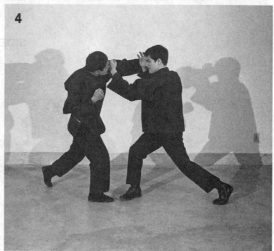

In the next illustration, Lee stands in the on-guard position preparing for the attack, as in photo 1. As the opponent initiates the attack, as in photo 2, Lee meets the left swing with a parry and counters by clawing the opponent's face, as in photo 3. Lee must time his forward movement and parry correctly to protect himself. In photo 4, Lee switches his hands smoothly so that he has time to deliver another blow—this time a backfist punch.

In the last illustration of the outside high parry, Lee uses the parry with a countering front kick. From the on-guard position, as in photos A and B, Lee parries a straight right. Without taking any step, he delivers a front kick to the opponent's groin almost at the same time, as in photo C. This is a safer parry than the preceding illustrations because he doesn't have to move in to reach his opponent because the leg is much longer than the arm.

When Lee can't find a partner, he practices alone on the wooden dummy. In the next three photos, Lee practices his parrying technique. In photo 1, he parries with his left hand and uses his right for countering. In photo 2, Lee's parrying hand crosses underneath his punching hand. In photo 3, Lee parries with his left hand and simultaneously releases a front kick.

The outside low parry against punches is performed almost similarly to the inside low parry except, in the former, the hand crosses over the body. The guard hand is used to protect the other side of the body against any low blow, as in photo A. Hence, the outside low parry has a greater circular motion than the inside low parry. Just like the inside low parry, its purpose is to deflect the oncoming blow downward.

JKD vs. Classical

The classical system uses the same blocking technique for all low-line blows. The hands just reverse their roles, as in photo B. The right hand is now used for blocking, and the left is used

for attacking. Like the other blocking techniques, there are two
distinct motions instead of one fluid, continuous motion, as in
jeet kune do.

In the next series of photographs, two classical fighters
confront each other, as in photo 1. Standing in the orthodox
stance, the fighter on the left throws a high punch, which is
blocked by his opponent, as in photo 2. The opponent follows
up with a right punch that the fighter on the left blocks, as in
photo 3, and counters with a straight right to the opponent's
solar plexus, as in photo 4.

The same technique is now presented against an unorthodox

(southpaw) opponent, using the JKD stance. Lee stands in the on-guard position, as in photo A, and as his opponent starts to attack, as in photo B, Lee readies to parry the blow with a slapping motion. In photo C, it shows the result of Lee's parry and his countering to the opponent's face.

Against an opponent who stands with his left lead (orthodox) forward, as in photo A, Lee quickly stops the thrust with a short shuffle backward and parries it as the opponent steps forward with a straight right. Lee's parry converts to trapping the opponent's hand just before he counters with a right to Lee's face, as in photo B.

The outside low parry is usually used against a kick that is directed below your chest with either a closed fist or an open hand.

The JKD and the classical parries seem similar, as in photos X and Y, but they differ in delivery. The JKD parry is executed with a semicircular, downward motion to deflect or control a kick. In the classical style, the block is performed with a downward, slanting, forceful motion to stop the kick in its path.

In the next series of photos, Lee illustrates how he defends against a lunging side kick. From the on-guard position, Lee readies for an attack, as in photo 1. As the opponent lunges forward to launch his kick, Lee synchronizes his backward movement with the opponent's, as in photo 2. He also retreats

just far enough to avoid the blow but stays close enough to ward off the kick, as in photo 3. Lee takes advantage of the situation by turning his opponent completely around so the opponent's back faces him. Lee then quickly employs a front kick to the groin, as in photo 4.

Against someone who is in a stance opposite of Lee's, as in photo 1, Lee moves backward with perfect timing to the attack. Lee has more time in this attack as his opponent uses his rear foot (the farthest foot) to deliver a front kick. Lee just moves a little backward in this attack because the penetration is not that deep, as in photo 2.

Lee parries the kick and prepares to defend against the next blow, as in photo 3. This time, he uses the inside low parry against the right punch, trapping his opponent's hand. Then he counters with his own straight right punch, as in photo 4.

Lee constructed his wooden dummy with an extra arm in the center of the structure strictly to practice his low-line parry, as in photo A.

Parrying vs. Blocking

To parry is merely to close the line or deflect the opponent's hand; it should not swing too far to the right or left but just enough to create advantageous openings necessary to counterfight.

Vary your parries to confuse the opponent. Don't let him set an attacking plan. Instead, keep him guessing. This will create hesitation on his part in launching his offensive maneuvers.

When there are a multitude of parries to be made, each parry must be completed, and your hand should be at the appropriate position before the next parry is made.

When there is a compound attack, the first parry is performed while moving your rear foot, and the second would be done in exactly the same time as you are shuffling backward from the second attack. Your rear foot must move before the attack and not after the delivery of the blow.

Parrying is more subtle than blocking, which is a more violent force, because it is used frequently to abuse the opponent's limbs. Blocking should be used infrequently and only when necessary because it can drain your energy. Besides, even if you block a well-delivered blow, it will still disturb your balance and create openings for your opponent. In the meantime, it prevents you from countering.

Chapter 10
Targets

Targets

Primary Targets

The two primary targets in fighting are the eyes and the groin, as in photo A below. A solid groin blow can quickly incapacitate or even cause death to a man no matter how physically powerful he is. Even a light blow can render a man unconscious.

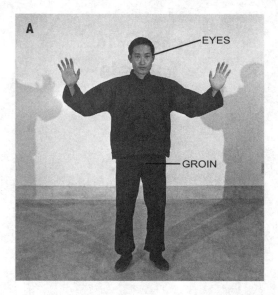

Some martial arts call such a vicious blow too cruel and inhumane. But Bruce Lee always felt that your main purpose in learning the martial arts or self-defense arts is self-protection or self-preservation.

"The meaning of 'martial' is 'warlike,'" he used to say. "We are not in a game; it's your life or his. And since you only have one life, take care of it the best you can."

"When you treat the martial arts like a sport," he said, "then you have established rules, which create weaknesses. Or when you attempt to be too civil, then you learn to resist for fear of hurting your adversary, and this can also weaken your defensive technique."

Many fighting arts, which became sports, establish rules that forbid certain dangerous techniques to the players. Consequently, most rules banned attacking the groin area and, as time went by, emphasis on guarding the groin area lessened to almost nothing. This is true in boxing, wrestling, judo and many styles of karate.

Because of the artificial protection today, many fighters do not know how to protect themselves from a kick to the groin, as in photo X. Even their stances are vulnerable to a fast frontal kick.

Lee saw this flaw and created his own stance, as in photo Y. In this stance, the groin area is well-protected by the lead thigh and by his adaptation of the shuffling footwork. It did not curtail his speed or freedom of footwork.

Another feature of jeet kune do is that the rear foot is rarely used for kicking except in a spin kick. The reason is that at that moment when the rear foot crosses the front, your groin area is exposed, especially with a roundhouse kick.

Finger-jabbing to the eyes (a primary target), as in photo 1, is also considered the first line in hand techniques for attacking

OTHER VITAL TARGETS

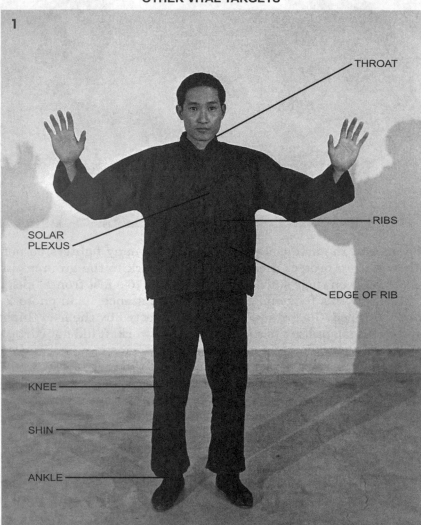

and defending, while the shin kick and knee kick is the first line in kick techniques. Eyes are a primary target because once blinded, you are almost helpless to defend yourself. It is referred to as the first line of offense or defense because finger-jabbing allows you an additional three or four inches in reach over a punch.

SIDE VIEW

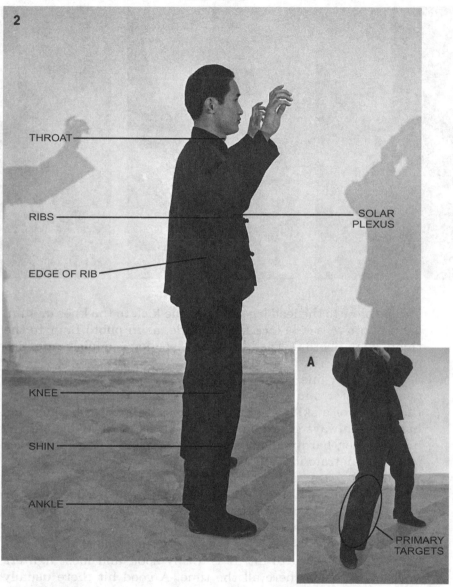

THROAT

RIBS

SOLAR
PLEXUS

EDGE OF RIB

KNEE

SHIN

ANKLE

PRIMARY
TARGETS

Vital Spots

Besides the primary targets, there are other vital spots in the human body, as in photos 1 and 2. The knee or shin kick is the first line of attack or defense because the leg allows you the longest reach, and the knee or shin generally are the targets closest to you.

The blow to the lead leg can be a side kick to the knee or shin, as in photo A, a side kick to the ankle, as in photo B, or to the thigh, as in photo C. The kick to the lead leg is a fairly safe kick if delivered correctly, as in photo 1.

The upper-line areas are harder to hit because they are usually better and easier for your opponent to guard. To hit the throat of a skilled fighter is almost impossible because his hands are always guarding it and because he tucks his chin to his shoulder, hardly allowing any opening. Sometimes a finger jab can penetrate it, as in photo X.

The rib cage is very vulnerable, especially if a blow is administered when the hand is held high. In such a position, the ribs are separated considerably and, as a result, are quite fragile to any kind of a sharp blow.

The solar plexus is one of the most vulnerable spots on your body, but it is hard to hit. It is a tiny spot, and most fighters have their hands there all the time. A good hit there usually discourages one from continuing to fight, but it is a rare occasion when a skilled fighter can be hit at that spot.

The jaw is a larger target than the throat, but it is an elusive target against a skilled fighter who can weave and duck. A fighter with good footwork can move away or just move his head away from the blow. By tucking his chin to his shoulder and by raising his shoulder to meet it, it becomes an inaccessible target to hit. Nevertheless, a hit to the jaw can be devastating, as in photo Z. There are more boxers knocked out from a hit to the jaw than to any other place. Besides, if a blow is delivered at a certain angle, as in photo Y, the jaw can easily be broken.

The science of fighting is not just to hit your opponent's body but to hit him at the most vulnerable spot. Better to finish a fight with one punch than with several.

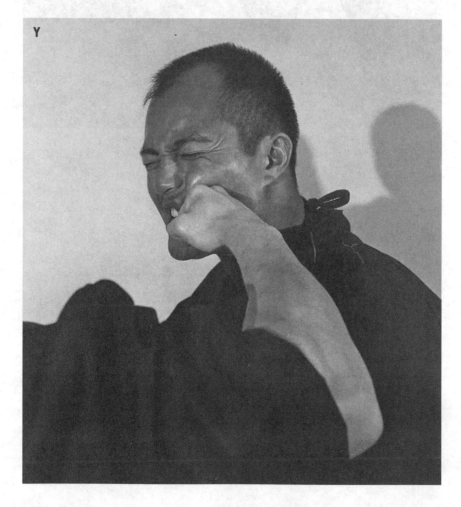

Y

Z

Correct Use of Arsenals

You also have to learn to hit without injuring yourself. Your fist must be formed properly or you can injure your thumb, fingers or your wrist. If you punch or kick correctly, you will not hurt yourself even if you miss your target and hit a harder substance.

In delivering a side kick, use the edge or flat of your foot to make contact with the target, as in photo A. Occasionally, you may be able to use your heel, as in photo B. If you are wearing shoes, the point of contact for a front kick can be the toe, as in photo C, the ball of your foot, as in photo D, or your instep, as in photo E. But if you are barefoot, avoid using your toes, and use caution when using the ball of your foot. The safest part to use is your instep. Sometimes the inside portion of your foot is employed, as in photo 1, but it's usually used for sweeps.

The strategy of fighting depends on the vulnerable spots that you must protect as well as the areas most easily within reach of your opponent.

Chapter 11
Sparring

Sparring

Contact sparring is the closest endeavor to real fighting. Unlike real fighting, there are limitations such as wearing protective gear and gloves as well as restrictions in the use of certain offensive techniques. Until man invents better equipment and methods, this is the most practical way to train today.

Bruce Lee always emphasized the importance of sparring. "A fighter who trains without sparring is like a swimmer who hasn't immersed in the water," he used to say.

There are shortcomings in modern fighting sports. In Western boxing, the participants have the inclination to become reckless because of the protective rules in the sport. They are restrained from using certain punches, prohibited from hitting below the belt and are not allowed to use their feet to kick.

Those who participate in Oriental martial arts tournaments, such as karate, are being overprotected by the noncontact practice of stopping the blows several inches from the body even though the full body is the target. This practice hurts the participants' ability to judge distance. Besides, this artificial shelter keeps practitioners from learning to slip, duck, weave and use the other defensive tactics found in boxing.

In real or total fighting, all the elements must be employed to be effective. You must use distance as a protective maneuver and all the evasive techniques of close fighting.

The science of fighting is the ability of one to outsmart and outmaneuver his opponent—to hit him without getting hit. In fighting, a good offense is the best defense, as in many other sports. A good fighter should beat his opponent to the punch with lightning-fast leads or outkick him with his quick lead foot. He attacks with deception. He creates openings for himself by his command of techniques that lead his opponent into a quandary. He must deliver proper kicks and punches instinctively so his mind is free for strategy.

Although sparring protective gear is cumbersome and weighty, it is the best way to gain some experience in simulated fighting conditions. The headgear will affect your vision, and the gloves will be cumbersome and heavy, but you must continue to use good posture and technique. You must be careful not to fall into a habit of careless defense while wearing the protective gear.

Stance

Keep your hands at the proper position, as in photo A. They should not be too low, as in photo B, because this leaves openings to your face and upper body. By keeping your hands too high, as in photo C, the lower-line areas are open, and it also prevents you from delivering an effective straight fast punch without first repositioning your hands. Besides, it also blocks your vision. Standing too much to the side, as in photo D, prevents you from utilizing your rear hand for defense or offense. Being too square, as in photo E, hinders you from rapid forward or backward movement and also exposes your vulnerable groin area.

Punching from too wide a stance, as in photo A, weakens your blows because you cannot utilize the full rotation of your hip motion. You are also handicapped in penetrating or retreating quickly, and your front foot becomes an easy target for your opponent.

Sparring with your feet too close, as in photo B, upsets your balance and prevents you from delivering a strong punch. Do not throw a punch while leaning back, as in photo C, because there is absolutely no power in such a punch. A punch must be thrown with your body upright and in balance, with the weight shifting to the lead foot. If you ever have to lean backward, reposition your body properly before delivering the blow. Why throw a punch if it is not effective?

Another ineffective blow is hitting while backing away. Your weight has to be shifted forward to have force. In other words, step back, stop, then hit. After the punch, if you have to keep backing up, do the same routine: step back, stop, then hit.

It takes good sense of distance and ability to stop in your retreat instantly and unexpectedly. Learn to maneuver quickly from defense to offense and vice versa.

An easy habit to fall into is to punch with your body leaning too far forward, as in photo D. Throwing a punch in this awkward position is futile because you cannot exert enough power into the blow when you are off-balance.

Like a good Western boxer, a skilled fighter should be able to hit from any angle. Each punch prepares him to deliver the next. He is always in balance to shoot any kind of punch. The more skillful he becomes as he learns more effective combinations, the more different types of opponents he will conquer.

You have to learn to be patient while sparring. Don't deliver your blows until you are certain to hit your opponent. Step toward him when you punch to make contact. Hit as straight as possible, using your nose as the guide in the delivery. Don't overshoot your target because a miss leaves you out of position and makes you a target for an easy counterpunch, especially against a boxer who leads. Instead, beat him with lightning-fast leads and draw his counterpunches with feints so he will miss.

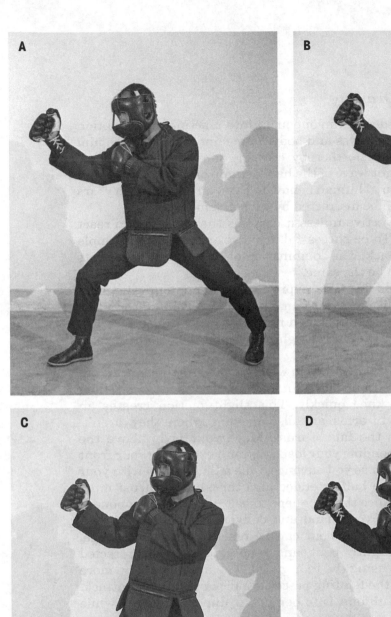

Feinting and Drawing

Feinting is to deceive an opponent into reacting to the motion of your hands, legs, eyes and body. Your feint should entice him to adjust his defense, thereby creating momentary openings. Reaction to a slight wave of the hand, stamp of the foot, a sudden shout, etc. is normal human behavior. Even an athlete with years of experience will be distracted by such a demonstration.

No feint is effective unless it compels the opponent to react to your wishes. To be successful, it must appear to be a simple movement of attack. The combination of hitting with the feints should appear to be the same.

A feint should be fast, expressive, threatening, changing and precise, followed by a clean, sharp blow. Feints are not as imperative against an unskilled fighter as against a skilled one. Between two evenly matched fighters, the one who is the master of the feint will be the winner.

There are several methods in which to execute the feint. From the on-guard position, move forward and, without hesitation, bend your lead knee quickly. This slight motion creates an illusion that your arms are also moving when they aren't. Another feint is the false thrust. Move your body above the waist by simply bending your lead knee and extending your front hand slightly. Then as you advance, take a longer step with your front foot and do a half-extended arm thrust. The thrust must appear real to induce the opponent to parry. When the opponent parries, disengage your hand and deliver the real thrust with either hand. If the opponent can be reached without a lunge, keep your arm slightly bent, and keep yourself well protected by shifting or by using the rear guard. The arm should be more fully extended if the feinting precedes a kick or a lunging attack. Another successful feint is to bend your upper body only while advancing.

The one-two feint can be employed "inside-outside and outside-inside" or "high-low and low-high" with one or both hands in combination. The initial feint must be long and deep but quick in order to draw the parry. The next response is to hit the opponent hard before he can recover. This feint is a "long-short" rhythm.

In the "long-short-short" rhythm, or the two-feint attack, the first feint must force the opponent to a defense. At that moment, the distance is closer for a short feint before delivering a short but real hit.

The "short-long-short" rhythm is a more advanced form of feinting. The opponent is not induced by the first feint, so the second feint is made long to mislead the opponent into thinking that it is the final thrust of a compound attack, thereby drawing him to parry. In this tactic, speed and penetration are the elements for success.

To prevent or lessen the chance of being countered heavily, leads should consistently be preceded by feints. But the continuous use of the same feint will defeat your purpose because the opponent can take advantage of this maneuver for a counterattack. Combinations of feints must be practiced until they become automatic. You must also train in the use of various types of feints to learn the different reactions from your opponents.

The immediate advantage of a feint is that from the outset, you can lunge to attack with a feint to gain distance. In other words, you can shorten the distance with a lunge and gain some time from the false attack by causing the opponent to react or hesitate.

The feints will be more successful after several real but simple attacks. This will confuse the less mobile opponent who will not know whether the attack is real or not. It may also excite a light-footed opponent to flee. But if an opponent doesn't respond to your feint, attack with straight or simple movements.

There are several ways of feinting: (1) Feint a jab to his face and hit him in the stomach, (2) feint a low side kick to his shin and deliver a hook kick to his head, (3) feint a jab to his face and deliver a side kick to his stomach, (4) and feint two jabs to his face, then hit his stomach, etc. Experiment with other feints to create openings.

Drawing is almost like feinting. Actually, feinting is a segment of drawing. In feinting, you attempt to deceive your opponent to react to your motion. In drawing, you leave part of your body uncovered to lead the opponent to attack that area. As he does, you are prepared to take a defensive measure and are ready to counter.

Drawing is also a strategy to lead the opponent to respond to your deception, and when he does, he is caught in a trap. For instance, you may retreat quickly to entice the opponent to lunge at an attack. As he does, you are ready to evade the attack and counter with a specific blow.

Body Motion

Speed and timing complement each other. A fast blow will not be powerful unless thrown with timing. In photo A, a punch is thrown ineffectively because of a poor sense of timing and distance.

You do not have to move with a rapid or jerky motion. Many times a smooth, unhesitant movement that is performed from rest without apparent preparation will hit the target because it is so unpredictable.

Timing is the capability to perceive the right moment for action, such as when the opponent is preparing or planning to move, when the opponent is in the midst of a movement, when the opponent is at a tense disposition, or when the opponent's concentration is in the doldrums.

Timing in fighting means perfect delivery as the opponent steps forward or is drawn into stepping forward. If your timing is off and you launch your blow too early, as in photo X, your energy is spent without any telling effect. If your delivery is too early, as in photo Y, then your blow is not too effective, as your force was still developing.

Timing a blow is the secret to powerful blows, but no one can be a really heavy hitter, even with perfect timing, unless he has complete confidence in his ability. Timing can be a mental problem, especially when your rhythm is broken. Your mind has difficulty in adjusting to the sudden interruption of your movement while it continues for a fraction of a second. This "half beat" is psychologically disturbing because you expect a full-count movement, but your opponent attacks halfway before the count is completed.

Speed is not the chief prerequisite when two fighters of equal ability and speed are matched. There is a slight advantage to

the first one who attacks, but there is a greater advantage to the one who knows how to break the rhythm. Even with only moderate speed, his half beat or unexpected movement can catch his opponent flat-footed because his rhythm or cadence is interrupted and because he can't adjust quickly enough.

Even with a pair of heavy gloves, you must continue to use basic training, such as nontelegraphing your blows. Your delivery will not be as efficient with the gloves on, but continue to practice this way because it will increase your proficiency in the technique—with or without gloves. Because your foot is not burdened with protective gear, kick naturally with speed and force in your sparring. Do not deliver a kick, as in photo 1, forewarning your opponent of your intention.

In boxing and in some Oriental martial arts, the hands are the primary and almost the only assets for offense and defense. But in other martial arts, the kicks definitely play a big part in strategic fighting. Unfortunately, many schools emphasize the foot too heavily and ignore the hand techniques.

Bruce Lee used to mention that the hands are the primary weapons for attacking and defending. The foot can be contained by the placement of your foot to the opponent's, as in photo A, and by closing in on him. But the hands are much more difficult to contain because they can be thrown from close quarters and from all angles.

There are other techniques besides parrying that you can use to defend against punches. Often it is better to use an alternative method, such as footwork, because you are usually in a better position to counter. Other alternatives are evasive tactics such as slipping, rolling, weaving and bobbing.

Slipping is evading a blow without moving out of countering range. Your timing and judgment must be perfect to be successful because the blow should miss by a fraction of an inch.

Although slipping can be executed either inside or outside a straight lead, the outside slip is preferred. It is safer to use and prevents the opponent from preparing for a counter. The idea is to turn your shoulder and body to the right or left so you can slip the opponent's blow over either one of your shoulders.

Slipping is a valuable technique in sparring because it allows you to use both hands for countering. You can hit harder moving inside a punch rather than blocking or parrying and then countering.

The small rotation of your heel is frequently the answer to successful slipping. To slip a right lead over your left shoulder from a right lead stance, raise your rear heel and rotate it clockwise, transferring your weight to the lead foot. Simultaneously bend your lead knee and turn your shoulder in the same clockwise direction so you will be in a position to retaliate.

To slip a lead over your right shoulder, raise your lead heel and rotate it counterclockwise, transferring your weight to the back foot. Simultaneously bend your rear knee and turn your shoulder in the same counterclockwise direction, preparing to counter with a right hook.

The science of bobbing and weaving is a valuable tactic to avoid blows and improve your defensive measures to counter with a more powerful punch, such as the hook. It provides you with access to the use of both hands for attacking whenever an opening develops.

Weaving in sparring involves moving your body from side to side and in and out. In the process, you also keep slipping straight leads directed toward your head. It makes an elusive target of your head because your opponent is uncertain about which way you will slip. Also, he is in a dilemma because he doesn't know which hand will deliver the punch.

To weave to the inside against a right lead, slip to the outside position first by dropping your head and body with a turn of your shoulder and bending of your knee. Close in under the completed punch and quickly resume your stance. The opponent's hand should be over your left shoulder. Keep your hands high and near your body. Then, without stopping your motion completely, swing your body to the inside position and engage your right hand to the opponent's left. Continue to weave and simultaneously counter with right and left punches.

To weave to the outside against a right lead, slip to the inside position by dropping your head and body with a twist of your upper body while bending your knee. Then move your head and body in a circular, counterclockwise motion so that the opponent's right hand is over your right shoulder. Keep your hands high and near your body. You should be at the outside position by then, standing in the on-guard stance.

Weaving is more difficult than slipping, but you must master slipping to be skilled in weaving. The key to weaving is to learn the art of relaxation.

Weaving is seldom used by itself. Usually it is accompanied by bobbing. Bobbing in fighting is usually referred to as moving the head constantly vertically rather than side to side. The way to bob is to barely sink under a swing or hook with a controlled motion. Your body should be in balance at all times so you can counterattack or slip straight punches even at the bottom of the bob. Don't counter or straight-down bob except to the groin. Keep your hands high and use your knees for motion.

The purpose of bobbing and weaving is to close in by sliding under the opponent's attack. Weave to employ counters of hard, straight punches or hooks. The master of bobbing and weaving is usually a hooking specialist who is able to dominate taller opponents. Like other skills in fighting, your weaving and bobbing must not be too rhythmic. You must keep the opponent confused at all times.

Rolling is moving your body in such a manner that the blow is wasted. For instance, against a straight punch and uppercut, you move backward. Against a hook, you move to your left or right. You do the same against a hammer, except you also move downward in a curved motion.

Always use evasive tactics with countering kicks or punches. Keep your eyes wide open because blows do come without much warning, and utilize your elbows and forearms for guarding. Evasive tactics, when used with hard hitting, can discourage an aggressor and turn the scuffle into grappling. When evasive maneuvers are not used, parry blows that are directed toward your head.

Skill in footwork can be developed greatly during sparring sessions because your feet can move freely in any direction. Although circling evasive tactics are not practiced too heavily in the Oriental martial arts, it is an important segment of close fighting when the use of kicks is not feasible.

In circling to your right, the lead foot is the axis to move your body around. The first step with your lead foot can be either long or short, depending on the situation. The shorter the step, the smaller the pivot. Keep your lead hand slightly higher than normal to prepare for a countering left punch.

Circling to the right is used to nullify a right lead hook, to keep the opponent off-balance and to deliver an advantageous left-hand counter. It is important to maintain your basic posture, move deliberately without any exaggerated motion and never cross your feet.

Circling to your left should be employed more frequently than the right because it is safer. You can stay out of range from rear, left-handed punches. But it is more difficult to do because it requires shorter steps to be exact in your movement.

The step-in and step-out are offensive maneuvers to create openings and are often used with a feint. The initial movement is to step in directly with your hands held high, creating an illusion of delivering a blow, then step out quickly before your opponent can counter. The strategy is to induce him into complacency so you can deliver a surprise attack.

A fighter with fast footwork and a good lead can impress on others that the art is simple and easy. He can make a slower opponent look bad by the process of hit and run. As the opponent moves in, he confronts him with a lead punch and quickly steps back. As the opponent pursues, he repeats the process—circling and moving in and out. Occasionally, he will meet his opponent head-on with a straight right or left, or with a combination.

Even while you are waiting in the on-guard position, your hands and body should be in a continuous, slightly bobbing motion. The motion can deceive and camouflage your attack as well as keep your opponent confused. The motion should not be overdone, or it will disturb your timing in attacking and defending.

In sparring, learn to be patient. Do not waste your energy by throwing a punch until you are almost certain that it will hit the target with power. Throwing a punch by overreaching, as in photo A (see page 232), is risky. First, your punch is too weak to do any damage even if it makes contact. Second, you place yourself in a precarious position against a counterpunch. And third, you have not locked your foot to the opponent's, allowing him freedom to deliver a hook kick to your unprotected groin.

A

Back your opponent into a corner or into the ropes before you attack. Throw accurate punches while you have him cornered. Missing too many times can easily wear you down.

For long-range sparring, jab with your lead, as in photo X, and cross with your rear. Judge your distance correctly before throwing a punch. For short-range sparring, use hooks, rear-hand body blows and uppercuts, but do not punch from too far out, as in photo Z. Punch through your opponent.

Weave as you hit. A hard punch can only be delivered from a solid base. Occasionally take a short step to the left by three or four inches with your rear foot when throwing a right lead punch. This will put more power in your punch, especially from long-range. Don't ever punch with your foot off the ground, as in photo A.

Have confidence when you spar. Don't move away from your opponent when you are delivering a punch, as in photo B. Your punch will lack power, and you will also reveal to your opponent a fear of being hit. Your timid action only increases his confidence and decreases your chance of fighting with strategy. Another bad gesture is to turn your head away from the attack, as in photo X. Such behavior leaves you open for additional attacks and prevents you from countering.

Bad Habits

During sparring is the time to learn your weaknesses and how to overcome them. It is too late in a real fight. You will be surprised to learn your pitfalls while sparring. Bad habits, such as standing with your feet parallel, may show up. You may only notice it when you find yourself easily being thrown off-balance, as in photo Y.

You may be retreating with your guard down, as in photo Z. But you will learn quickly to keep your guard up after you take several hard blows to your face.

There are so many variables in fighting that you cannot follow a stringent plan. You have to be flexible as different situations arise.

PART III
ADVANCED TECHNIQUES

Chapter 12
Hand Techniques for Offense
(Part A)

Hand Techniques For Offense

In jeet kune do, there are hardly any direct attacks. Practically all offensive maneuvers are indirect—performed after a feint or in the form of a counterattack. One can say that jeet kune do is built on feints and the actions connected to them.

A perfect attack is the blending of strategy, speed, timing, deception and keen judgment. A superior fighter strives toward mastering all these elements in his daily training.

The attack should be launched at your own volition, upon your opponent's action or upon his inaction. For instance, a successful attack can be delivered when your opponent is withdrawing his arm from the path in which you intended to attack. In other words, attack when the line is open instead of closed. Your opponent is moving in the opposite direction and he must reverse his direction or alter it substantially to counter your hit, allowing you more time to succeed.

Simple attacks will not always work against every opponent. You must learn to vary your attacks and defense. This will bother your opponent and also help you cope with various styles of fighters.

You must study your opponent. Take advantage of his weaknesses and avoid his strengths. For instance, if your opponent is good at parrying, you should first use a press, feint or beat before attacking to confuse him.

The method of attack is dictated by the form of defense. If your opponent is of your caliber, your attack will hardly be successful unless it outwits his defense. For instance, to deceive your opponent's hand defense, your hand offense is usually made of semicircular or circular movements. But an offensive circular movement will not work if it is countered with a simple or lateral motion of a parry. Therefore, your strike should be based on your anticipation of the opponent's reaction.

It is precarious to attack with anything that comes to mind or to launch yourself into complicated compound attacks that allow your opponent several chances to perform a stop-hit. The more complex the attack, the less you are likely to execute it with control. Therefore, your attacks should be simple.

But if your opponent is equal in speed and skill and has a good sense of distance, a simple attack may not score a hit. Against such an opponent, you have to use compound attacks and take advantage of distance.

A compound attack is a preliminary action, such as a feint, beat, etc., that launches before your real attack. The success of the compound attack depends directly on the parry of your feint or initial attack of your opponent. You have to study the opponent's reaction before applying the compound attack.

Compound attacks depend on timing and opportunity. Many compound attacks fail because the attacker doesn't time his feints correctly. They should be moving just slightly before the real attack. Compound attacks can be short, fast combinations or deep, fast and penetrative combinations.

A simple compound attack—just one feint or one preliminary action—has a better chance to score if it is executed on the opponent's preparation, especially if he is stepping forward. Against an opponent who has slow feet or is exhausted, use the double-lead.

While attacking, you should act and look as fierce as a wild animal to psych out your opponent. You should attack with determination but not recklessness. It is risky to attack halfheartedly.

Even with good techniques, you can be frustrated by a skilled opponent's defensive measures. Therefore, you should time your attack perfectly so your opponent cannot evade your blows. The following are some of the hand techniques used in jeet kune do.

Leading Finger Jab

The leading finger jab, as in photo X, like the shin or knee side kick, is the first line of offense or defense. It allows you an additional three to four inches in reach and provides a fast strike because it travels only a short distance to the target.

Like other skilled movements, it must be practiced when you are fresh. Whenever you are fatigued, your tendency is to use sloppy motions for finesse and generalized efforts for specific actions. By using continuous, sloppy movements, your proficiency is retarded and may even retrogress. Anytime you are exhausted, change your drills from skill-based to endurance-type exercises.

The finger jab is executed from an on-guard position, as in photo 1. Just before thrusting, the fingers of your striking hand should be extended, as in photo 2. You should complete your strike directly in front of your nose, as in photo 3 and not like in photo A, which leaves an opening at the upper-line area.

To attack directly with a finger jab against a skilled fighter is quite difficult. Bruce Lee always used it with a feint first.

For instance, Lee stands in the on-guard position as he faces his opponent, as in photo 1, who is in a similar position. He then feints low by crouching slightly and moves forward as if to attack the opponent's midsection. This causes the opponent to lower his guarding rear hand, as in photo 2. As soon as the opening develops, Lee quickly thrusts his fingers into the opponent's eye, as in photo 3. Notice that Lee places his right foot next to the opponent's to prevent any retaliation from the opponent's foot. A feint is a preliminary motion to entice your opponent to react. You draw him to parry to a particular line, then you deliver an attack using another line or path.

Against an opponent in a left lead stance, as in photo A, Lee fakes with his right-hand lead to lower the opponent's leading hand, as in photo B. In this instance, Lee is only concerned about the opponent's lead hand because it is obstructing his path to

the target. Once the obstruction is removed, Lee quickly takes advantage of the moment with a quick thrust to the opponent's eye, as in photo C. In this attack, Lee is able to accomplish his technique from a farther distance. The feint can also be a low shin kick to disturb the opponent's composure. Besides using it as a feint, it also prevents the opponent from delivering a kick.

Whether it is a jab, punch or kick, speed is so important when you want to lead an opponent. You must have speed over him rather than let him keep up or catch up to you.

Speed and timing should work together. You should be able to dictate the rhythm to your opponent by either speeding up or slowing down your movements. Another way is to establish a natural rhythm and then suddenly attack when your opponent is in the doldrums and his motion begins to drag.

Economy of motion and keeping your muscles flexible can

increase your speed. A fault of most novice competitors is that they try too hard to finish the match quickly and begin to press and hasten their actions. This only makes them less effective because the tension causes unnecessary muscular contractions that act as brakes—reducing their speed and expending their energy.

A higher performance is obtained when an athlete is free and unrestrained, rather than when he tries to force or drive himself. When a runner is going as fast as he can, he should not feel that he ought to be going faster.

Another effective technique is to change your timing, like slowing down instead of speeding up your movement, just before impact. In other words, there is a moment of pause in the launching strike's forward path, compelling your opponent to open a vulnerable line as he is thrown out of timing.

Timing may mean success or failure in your offensive and defensive techniques. An attack or counter should occur at the moment your opponent appears inept. Attacks should come when your opponent is engrossed in preparing his offense because he is momentarily concentrating more on his attack than his defense. Other opportune times for attacking occur when there is an absence of touch during an engagement or transition to an engagement, and when the opponent is in motion—stepping forward, backward or side-to-side—because he cannot intuitively change direction until his action is completed.

It takes a great deal of concentration and practice to develop this awareness of your opponent's weak moment. You must also learn not to be trapped by a misleading, false rhythm emanated by a clever fighter. Rather, you should work to develop your ability to dictate the fighter's rhythm yourself, enabling you to land an unexpected blow.

In broken rhythm, speed is no longer the primary element in the success of an attack or counterattack. There is a tendency, if the rhythm has been well established, to continue in the sequence of the movement. Each man is "motor-set" to continue in that sequence. If you can break this set rhythm by a slight hesitation or an unexpected movement, you can now score an attack or counterattack with only moderate speed. Your opponent is motor-set to continue with the previous rhythm, and before he can adjust himself to the change, he will be hit by you. Broken rhythm will often catch your opponent mentally and physically off-guard for defense.

Leading Straight Right

The leading straight is the "bread and butter" punch of jeet kune do, as in photo 1. It is a reliable, offensive weapon because the delivery is short, accurate and quick.

It can be a powerful blow if you twist your hips just a split second before delivery. The blow should land in front of your nose, as in photo A and not like photo B. Your guard hand should be close to defend your head against any counterpunch. The blow should land directly on the opponent's face, as in photo C.

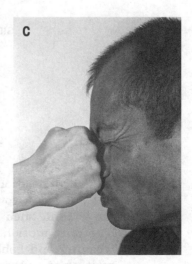

1

FRONT VIEW

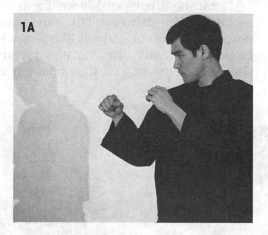

1A

SIDE VIEW

The straight right should be delivered directly from the on-guard position, as in photos 1 and 1A. Your hand should not telegraph your intention before delivery. Do not add extra movement, such as withdrawing your fist just before delivery. The only motion should come as a consequence of your slight weaving and bobbing while you are looking for an opening or waiting to counter. Punch straight out, as in photos 2 and 2A,

with your fist in the vertical position. Your rear hand should
be in the guard position, ready to block any blow. By extending
your shoulder into the blow, you can increase your reach by as
much as four inches and not reduce the impact of your punch.
However, you must use your body properly and punch through,
as in photos 3 and 3A.

Against someone standing closer to him, as in photo 1, Lee delivers a quick, straight right without telegraphing his intention, as in photo 2. But against someone standing farther away, as in photo A, or who has the inclination to retreat, Lee penetrates a little deeper to launch his blow, as in photo B.

In all hand techniques, the hand moves before the foot. Delivery must be economical from any angle and from any distance. In an attack, the movements must be as concealing or as slight as ever, especially with your hands, to inhibit the

opponent from reacting into a defensive or countering measure.

You must understand that there is an opening for every lead, a counter for each opening, and a block or parry for each counter. You must know when and how to use the lead with some security to be a master of this attack.

Lead to Body

Although the leading right to the body is not necessarily a heavy blow, it can be used effectively to bother your opponent and bring his guard down. If the punch is driven into the solar plexus, it can do real damage to the opponent, as in photo A. In photo 1, Lee demonstrates a full-view lead to the body.

A

1

FRONT VIEW

SIDE VIEW

To execute the leading right to the body, stand in the on-guard position, as in photo 1 and 1A. Then drop your body down and step forward, as in photos 2 and 2A. Your front leg should be slightly bent, and your rear leg should be more flexible. As you

strike in at an angle, your chin should naturally move into your right shoulder. At the punch's full extension, your rear hand should guard your face, as in photos 3 and 3A, and your weight should shift almost completely to your front foot.

It is important that you follow through with your punch. Try to sink your body to the level of the target so your blow will be delivered slightly upward or almost horizontally. This delivery position is safer and more effective.

Lee stands in the on-guard position against a right-lead opponent, as in photo 1. He moves in quickly with a blow to the midsection, simultaneously using his left hand to block a high lead punch, as in photo 2.

Most people are weak in their low-line defense, and blows toward that section are effective especially during a disengagement. A disengagement is a single movement that happens when the opponent's hand passes from the line of engagement into the opposite line, i.e. throwing a hit from a closed line into an open line. Timing is very important because you must start your attack as the opponent's arm is moving across the line or in the opposite direction.

Against a left-lead opponent, as in photo A, Lee feints with his lead hand to draw his opponent's hands upward, as in photo B. As soon as the opening develops, Lee drives a hard lead right to the solar plexus, as in photo C. He is now in position to deliver a left-to-right combination.

To defend against a straight lead from a right stance, you can do several things. First, keep your left hand open and hold it slightly higher than normal while keeping it weaving. As the opponent's punch is launched toward your face, lean a little to your left and parry the blow with your left hand by slapping his wrist and forearm. No amount of strength is required to deflect even a powerful strike. The deflection will leave your opponent off-guard and off-balance for a quick counter to his face or body. Second, swing to your left by stepping in with your right foot and letting go a hard right to the body or face. Third, move to the right by stepping in with your right foot and throwing a strong left to the body or head in a cross-counter. Fourth, take a step back and counter as you move forward.

Straight Left

The straight left is a powerful blow if delivered properly, as in photo X. It is used as a counter or as part of a combination. More power is generated than in a lead punch because you are standing farther away and can increase the momentum of the blow before it makes contact with its target. Furthermore, you have the full use of your body to put behind the punch.

X

But for most right-handers, using the left is unnatural, especially when thrown from a distance. To develop skill in punching with your left, practice with it constantly on the heavy bag until it is just as proficient as the other hand.

To throw a straight left, stand in the on-guard position, as in photos 1 and 1A. Rotate your hips clockwise, pivoting mostly on your flexed rear foot, as in photos 2 and 2A. Your weight should shift to your front foot, and your lead hand should be drawn to your face for protection, as in photos 3 and 3A. Your punch

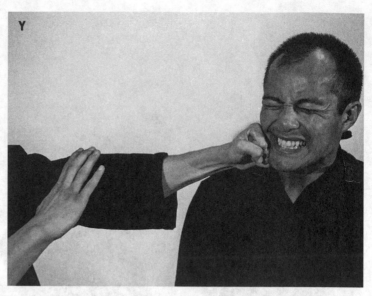

should be delivered straight in front of your nose and not like in photo X, where your upper line is left unguarded after the delivery. Your target can be anywhere on your opponent's head, but the most vulnerable spot is the side of his jaw, as in photo Y. But do not aim at the head all the time. Sometimes aim at the opponent's centerline and drive through it.

Against someone in the same stance as you, i.e. right lead, as in photo 1, Lee creates an opening with a feint, as in photo 2. First he throws a right by stepping out with his right foot. The opponent responds by raising his hands to meet the blow. Just before Lee's right connects and obstructs the opponent's sight, he delivers a straight left to the opponent's face, as in photo 3. This delivery is done with a twist of his hip to the right as he pivots on the sole of his left foot. The pivot should be done sharply with a snap of the hip and completed with a snap of the left shoulder.

If your opponent steps back without parrying or blocking, it is often a good maneuver to renew the attack, aiming at an advanced target such as the shin or knee. It is also effective against someone who opens himself up by retreating with wide movements, or against someone who tries to parry but is off-balance and caught in a moment of hesitation.

Against an opponent who places his weight on the rear foot instead of taking a short step back, attack that rear foot. The effectiveness of a renewed attack depends highly on your knowledge of the way your opponent fights. It can hardly succeed without preliminary plans. You must also have good footwork for a quick forward recovery and an ability to keep your opponent off-balance.

The techniques of a renewed attack are a straight thrust and a feint, or a beat or trap done in combinations. An attack by combination is usually comprised of setups. It is a series of punches or kicks delivered naturally and to more than one line. The purpose of the attack is to draw or force your opponent into a precarious position for a finishing blow.

Combination blows come in certain sequences. For instance, it is natural to punch to the head first and then punch to the body with a straight punch and then a hook, a right hook and

then a straight left, or a straight left and then a right jab.

There are also triple blows in combinations. For instance, you can get your opponent by launching two blows to his body after a slip. This generally results in your opponent dropping his guard and leaving an opening for the final and third blow.

There is also the safety triple in which the first blow and the final blow land on the same target. For example, if the initial punch is to the body and the second to the jaw, then the last punch should target the body, as in photos A to D. Lee uses a

feint to open up his opponent. He then strikes his opponent with a rear cross to the body, followed by a lead hook to the head, and finishes by throwing the rear cross back to the body.

Often, the left or rear thrust is used as a countering blow. This can be done by drawing your opponent to lead an attack with a punch. When he does, duck your head slightly and step inside his right lead, letting it slip over your left shoulder. Then throw your left punch with power by snapping your left shoulder. Keep your eyes constantly on his left hand, stopping it with your right if he uses it.

Against someone in the opposite stance, as in photo 1, Lee feints with his right, as in photo 2, then quickly delivers a straight left to the opponent's face, as in photo 3. Notice in photo 2 (see page 259) and photo 2 (opposite page), that Lee doesn't have to penetrate too deeply when the opponent stands in the opposite position from him.

A decoy or false attack is employed not to hit but to draw or entice your opponent to attack along a specific line so you can parry the blow and counter. The attack is not a lunge but just a slight movement of the foot or body to create a response.

Chapter 13
Hand Techniques for Offense
(Part B)

Hand Techniques for Offense

Although speed is important, too many fighters put too much emphasis on it. When a fighter's offensive blows fail, often times it's because he uses the wrong strikes and blames his failures on a lack of speed.

A fighter must use the proper strikes at the right time against his opponent. To use the correct strikes, he has to study his opponent's style from different angles and study his opponent's tactics and timing. Included in this section are some of the strikes that are used in jeet kune do.

1

Straight Left to the Body

The straight left blow to the body, as in photo 1, like the straight left (see page 256), is powerful and can be used as a counter, after a feint with the leading hand, or even in combination. Like the leading jab (see page 272) or leading straight, the body should follow the punch.

It is a punishing punch and can be applied with some safety because you are in a crouch position when you deliver the punch. The opportunity to use this punch is also frequent because it is one of the best counters against an opponent who stands in an opposing (opposite) lead stance, exposing his right side.

It is also effective in drawing your opponent's guard down, and it has been used triumphantly against tall fighters. This technique should be used primarily against an opponent who keeps his rear hand high to protect his face when delivering a lead punch.

The punch is delivered almost like the straight left, except the blow is directed to the midsection, as in photo A, or to the

solar plexus. From an on-guard right-lead position, as in photos 1 and 1A, bend your knee slightly and keep your rear leg flexed, as in photo 2. Your lead hand draws toward your face, as in photo 2A, and now becomes the guard as you thrust your left hand forward. Your weight shifts to the front foot as you pivot on your back foot. For a more powerful blow, you can step slightly to the right as the blow is thrown. When returning to your original

position, keep your lead shoulder raised to protect yourself against an opponent's left cross or left hook.

Meanwhile, your right guard hand should be open and held close to your face by the time your thrust is completed, as in photos 3 and 3A. Sink your body so the blow can be thrown slightly upward or almost horizontal to your target. Don't expose your upper-line area when using this punch, as in photo Y.

Against an opponent in a matching (same) stance, as in photo 1, Lee creates an opening with a deep, false attack, drawing the opponent to raise his hands to meet the attack, as in photo 2. Then Lee quickly sinks his body and smashes a left to the midsection, as in photo 3. His head is down along his left shoulder and well-protected against a counter.

Against an opponent who stands in the opposite stance, as in photo A, Lee's penetration is not too deep. Instead, he feints a lead right to the opponent's face, as in photo B, while at the same time stepping in closer. When the opponent commits himself to

the feint, Lee drives a hard straight left to his body, as in photo C. At this point, Lee's right hand is up and open, and his elbow is down to guard against any counters.

Sometimes, instead of feinting to draw the opponent's lead, just wait for him to lead. Then quickly attack when there is an opening to his body. A body attack does have an advantage over a head attack because your target is bigger and less mobile.

To stop a rear-thrust counter to your body, just leave your front arm across your body and raise your lead shoulder in case your opponent throws a double-hit or "loop" punch.

Lead Jab

The jab is not a powerful punch, but it is useful because it keeps your opponent off-balance and from becoming "set." It is a fast, snappy punch and not a push. Your hand should be held, launched and returned high to offset a rear-hand counter. The arms should be relaxed and should sink instead of pulling back when brought back to the on-guard position.

It is practical to launch more than one jab because the second one has a good chance to land if the previous one was delivered with economy. The subsequent one is also a cover-up for a missed jab. A multitude of jabs can be thrown to keep your opponent on the defensive as you steadily press him, offering him no rest.

Backfist

The backfist, as in photo 1, is one of the most surprising punches you can deliver because it is fast, accurate and nontelegraphic. It can be launched from either the on-guard

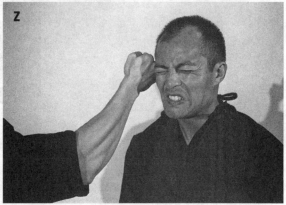

position or even when you are standing nonchalantly with your hands hanging loosely by your hips. In the latter position, you are in a nonthreatening position and able to sneak a blow in before your opponent is prepared to defend himself.

The delivery of the leading backfist should come directly from the front hand without telegraphing it, as in photo X. The blow should come overhand and not like in photo Y, in which the hand is chambered and swung horizontally. The blow can also be directed anywhere on your opponent's face, but the temple is the best target to aim at, as in photo Z.

FRONT VIEW

SIDE VIEW

From the on-guard position, as in photos 1 and 1A, the leading backfist is delivered in a vertical, semicircular motion, as in photos 2 and 2A. Your bodyweight shifts to the front as your

rear hand simultaneously moves slightly downward to protect against any kicks as well as any punches to your head or body, as in photos 3 and 3A. Open your rear hand for parrying.

Against an opponent in the right lead stance, as in photo 1, Lee traps the opponent's arm with his right hand and places his front foot on the opponent's right foot to prevent him from kicking, as in photo 2. Then Lee quickly switches his hands, using his left to immobilize the opponent's right arm and his right hand to apply a backfist as he steps in, as in photo 3.

Against someone standing in the left lead position, as in photos A to C, Lee uses the same technique as in the prior illustrations.

From the on-guard position, as in photo A, Lee uses his right hand to trap the opponent's left hand, as in photo B. He places his lead foot next to the opponent's lead foot to prevent a countering kick. Then Lee swiftly moves in as he switches his hands, using his left for grabbing and his right to deliver a blow, as in photo C. Notice that Lee uses his left hand to jerk his opponent toward him as he simultaneously delivers a semicircular blow.

Trapping, or immobilizing, is a method of stopping your opponent from moving certain parts of his body, and it guarantees you safety while you launch your attack. For instance, one hand can be used for pinning an opponent and the other for striking him. It can also be used as a protective maneuver when you are countering or slipping an attack. Trapping is basically used to collide with the opponent's line of attack before engagement.

Trapping, deflecting, beating or engaging the hand of your opponent will cause him to withdraw or limit his reaction, or force him to parry too soon or lose control of his performance.

The foot can also be used to immobilize your opponent from kicking.

You can limit your opponent from executing a successful stop-hit if you deflect or trap his hand while stepping forward. When trapping, you should cover your lines or use other means as guards and keep your movement tight. Also, as you are trapping or have already trapped your opponent's hand, use a stop-hit or timed hit if there is a disengagement.

Hook Punch

The hook, as in photo X, is a good countering or follow-up blow because it is basically a short-range weapon that catches the opponent as he moves in. The lead hook can also be used as a lead when your opponent fails to move out of your way. But usually this punch is used faster after a straight lead like a jab or after some other tactics. For instance, it can be used after feinting a cross to obtain leverage and distance.

The hook should not be thrown in a wide, looping way but

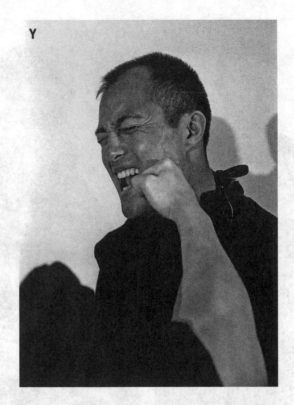

Y

should be easy, snappy and loose. In hooking loosely, the whip of the arm is the result of the body turning away from the arm until the play of the shoulder joint is used to the limit. Then the arm must follow the turning body. If done suddenly, this causes the arm to whip forward like an arrow from a bow.

The hand should not telegraph your intention by withdrawing or lowering before delivery. It is not necessary to pull your hand back like many boxers do. There is enough power without doing that if you use your footwork properly. Keep your lead heel raised outward so that the body can pivot easily. The weight of the body should shift to the opposite side from the punching hand. If you are throwing a lead hook, you must step in with the punch in order to make contact.

In a lead hook, keep your rear hand high to shield your face while your rear elbow protects your side. The hook should be thrown from an on-guard position to deceive your opponent, and after it is completed, you should return to the same position. Keep the lead shoulder high for full leverage when you hook to the side of the opponent's chin, as in photo Y.

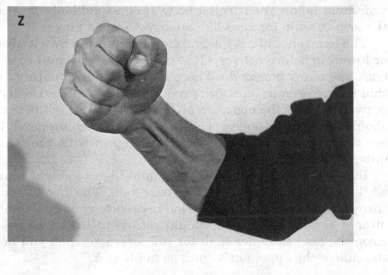

Minimize your motion so that your action is just enough to have the maximum effect without hooking uncontrollably. If you exaggerate the outside hook, it will turn into a swing, as in photo X. Instead you must keep it tight, as in photo Y. Besides, if you open a hook, you also reduce your defenses. The more sharply your elbow is bent, as in photo Z, the tighter and more explosive the hook. Keep your arm a little more rigid just before impact.

To deliver the hook from the on-guard position, as in photo 1, keep your rear guard high, as in photo 2, and your lead heel raised outward to pivot with ease. Then swiftly rotate your hips counterclockwise as you deliver the hook, as in photo 3, shifting your weight to your rear foot. Throw the blow with snap while concentrating on your speed. Like the other blows, drive your hook through the opponent. The greatest difficulty in the hook is throwing the punch with complete control of your body.

The lead hook should be used wisely. Against a clever, defensive fighter, this may be the only way to penetrate his defense or open it up by forcing him to use other tactics. But the hook is mostly effective when you move in or out. If you are against an

opponent who throws an overreaching straight punch or swings his arm, the hook is valuable.

Against an opponent in the same stance, as in photo 1, the lead hook is often delivered when he has lowered his rear-hand guard, as in photo 2, or after he has thrown a lead jab. The punch is delivered with the weight on the rear foot, the hips rotating and the ball of the raised front foot pivoting, as in photo 3.

Against an opponent standing in the opposite position, as in photo A, Lee employs a false attack by crouching slightly and feinting a rear straight thrust, as in photo B. As the opponent drops his lead to block the punch, Lee retaliates with a high hook to his jaw, as in photo C.

The hook is a natural punch when combined with a side step. You are moving obliquely, and your direction facilitates an easy swing at the opponent. Paradoxically, when your opponent is sidestepping, a hook is the practical punch to deliver, too.

The lead hook is also good in close-quarters fighting. The blow is thrown from the side or outside the opponent's range of vision. Besides, it can also go around the guard, which is an important offense, especially after the opponent is shaken up by a straight blow.

The hook to the body is more damaging in close-range fighting. Additionally, the body is an easier target—larger than the jaw and less mobile. To close in, feint to the head. Then swiftly step forward with the front foot and throw your lead hook into his midsection or the nearest target. The groin is a good target because it is harder to protect than, for instance, the jaw. When delivering the punch in close, duck to the opposite side of the hand that is throwing the hook. To do this, you have to bend your front knee so your shoulder will be almost the same level with the striking point. Retain your balance by keeping the toe of your back foot well extended. Keep your guard hand constantly close to your face.

Even though straight punches are recommended for medium-distance fighting, the hook should be used against an opponent who is blocking, evading or countering the straight punches. Vary your punches from high to low to high and from a single strike to a combination.

The rear hook is an asset for close fighting, especially when you are breaking away or when the opponent is breaking away from you. This punch can also distract the opponent away from the lead hook.

The hook is mastered by training on a small speed bag. Hit it sharply without twisting your body into distortion. To defend against it, do not move away from the opponent but move into the hook and let it pass around your neck.

Uppercut

The uppercut is used in close-quarters fighting. The blow, an upward scooping motion with the closed palm facing you, can be administered with either the lead or rear hand. The uppercut is almost useless against a fast, upright boxer who uses long lead jabs to your face. But it is a natural technique against someone who puts his head down and charges, swinging wildly.

To deliver an effective short uppercut, keep your knees bent before striking and straighten them as you throw the punch. At impact, you should be on your toes and leaning slightly backward. The weight should be on your left foot if the blow is a right uppercut and vice versa if the blow is a left uppercut.

Against a right-lead opponent, use your left hand to trap the opponent's right arm as you deliver a right-lead uppercut. To execute the left-rear uppercut, the lead hand is drawn back to protect your head and also to be prepared for countering. The left hand should be lowered so the inertia of the blow is across and up.

Chapter 14
Attacks With Kicks

Attacks With Kicks

In attacking, the best kicks to use are the quick, fast ones. A kick has to be delivered before your opponent can defend against or move away from it. Be sure your opponent doesn't take advantage of your commitment. Attempt to psych out your opponent with punishing blows while inflicting sharp pain.

In your training, be aware of your delivery, landing and recovery. Use kicks that snap from the knee for more power, and combine both the knee and the hip for more speed.

Learn to control your body so you can kick from a high, low or ground level while you are in motion—advancing, retreating, circling to the left or to the right.

Leading Shin and Knee Kick

It is natural for most martial artists to use or rely on their feet as their initial weapon for attacking because the leg is stronger and longer than the arm. In jeet kune do, the low side kick to the shin or knee, as in photo A, is used initially in the

first encounter. The kick is explosive whether it is thrusting or snapping, and it can wreck the opponent's knee with one blow. It is a good technique to bridge the gap in order to employ combinations. Even if the kick is not thrown excessively, it still can discourage an opponent from taking the initiative and keep him at a distance.

Against someone standing in the same stance, as in photo 1, Lee sweeps his lead hand upward to distract his opponent, as in photo 2. Lee quickly lunges forward to deliver his low side kick to the knee, forcing his opponent to the ground, and continues to kick without letting up, as in photo 3. Notice how far Lee stands from his opponent when the kick is delivered.

Against someone standing in an opposite stance, as in photo 1, Lee uses the same approach by sweeping his hand upward, as in photo 2. He then quickly drives his side kick to the opponent's left knee as in photo 3. Notice that Lee approaches the opponent with his eyes upon the opponent's face and not on his knee or the target area. Lee does this to camouflage his intentions and to keep his opponent from guessing his intention.

Leading Side Kick

The side kick is the most powerful blow in jeet kune do, as in photo A. It is so strong that, many times, even a block will not prevent it from knocking down or hurting your opponent. The kick can be launched from a medium distance, but there is more power if it is launched from farther out because you can increase your momentum before contact.

A

Against someone in the same stance, as in photo 1, Lee raises his hand from a medium distance, as in photo 2, keeping his other hand down to protect from a countering kick. He quickly delivers a side kick to the opponent's ribs, as in photo

3, hurling him backward, as in photo 4. Although the kick is powerful, it is quite difficult to hit your opponent solidly if he is a defensive fighter. The defensive measures are used by the opponent to either move far enough away from the point of

penetration or sidestep away from the kick. Another defensive measure is to parry the blow for a chance of grabbing it.

Against someone in the opposite stance, as in photo A, Lee just moves in, studying the reaction of the opponent, as in photo B.

When the opponent starts to back off from the attack, Lee lunges without any hesitation, as in photo C. Moving faster than the opponent, Lee delivers his side kick, as in photo D.

In the series of photos on the opposite page, as the opponent stands in the opposite stance, as in photo 1, Lee tries his familiar hand-raised feint as he moves forward, as in photo 2. But this time, the opponent refuses to respond, so Lee changes his tactics and uses a high side kick over the opponent's guarding hands, as in photo 3.

Hook Kick

The hook kick is the most dominating kick in jeet kune do, as in photo A, because it is easy to hit your opponent with. The way the kick is delivered gives you more opportunities to attack and, at the same time, offers you security when at a medium-fighting distance. It can be delivered quickly and is very versatile. It can be aimed at the head, midsection and even the groin.

Against an opponent in a right lead stance, as in photo 1, Lee first feints a knee kick, drawing the opponent's guarding hand down, as in photo 2. Once the opponent reacts to the feint, Lee sends a high hook kick to his face, as in photos 3 and 3A.

The feint must be impressive enough to create a response from the opponent. The number of feints should be limited to be effective. It is risky to try an attack with more than two feints. The more complicated the maneuvers of the compound attack, the less the probability of success.

The feint is one method of gaining distance. Your first feint should shorten the distance by at least one-half between you and your opponent. Your next motion should cover the last half of the distance. Your feint should be prolonged to give your opponent ample time to react, but not prolonged too long so he has time to block your attack. You have to be just ahead of it. All your motions should be slight and just enough for a response.

BIRD'S EYE VIEW

In this next series of encounters against an opponent with a right lead stance, as in photo 1, Lee tries the raising-hand distraction to open up the midsection area, as in photo 2. When the opponent responds to the bluff, Lee delivers a hook kick to his left side, as in photo 3.

Against an opponent in the opposite stance, as in photo A, Lee lowers his body, as in photo B, and fakes a low hook kick to draw the opponent's left hand to protect his low-line area, as in photo C. When he does, Lee delivers a high hook kick to his head, as in photo D. This hook kick is easier to execute against someone who is in the same stance as yours.

Spin Kick

The spin kick, as in photo A, is used cautiously in jeet kune do because, against a defensive or less aggressive fighter, you may be caught with your back to him while you are turning. Nevertheless, it is a valuable kick against an unwary opponent who keeps rushing you.

The spin kick is one of the most difficult to perform because it can leave you off-balance while revolving. Hitting the target can also be a problem because, for a moment, you have to take your eyes off it and still hit it while your body is turning.

The spin kick is used mostly as a counter, but from time to time, it can be used as an attack to surprise your opponent.

Against someone in the same stance, as in photo 1, Lee sweeps
his hand upward as a distraction as he moves toward his
opponent. Then, at the right moment, he pivots on his right
foot and rotates his body suddenly, as in photo 2. He tries to
keep his eyes on his opponent to judge his distance. Before the
opponent can react, Lee delivers a spin kick to his midsection,
as in photo 3. Some martial artists employ the spin kick in a
sweeping or slapping motion so the blow is projected from the

side. But in jeet kune do, it is more of a thrust, with the blow hitting the target's front directly.

To apply a high spin kick against his opponent in the same stance, as in photo A, Lee fakes with his lead hand, as in

photo B. But the opponent doesn't respond to the gesture in photo B, so Lee quickly pivots on his right foot and sends a high kick to the face, as in photo C. This drives him back, as in photo D.

Against someone in the opposite stance, as in photo 1, Lee sweeps his hand, as in photo 2. He quickly turns his body completely, as in photo 3, to drive a spin kick between the opponent's guard, forcing him off his feet, as in photo 4.

Although the spin kick works best against an unwary, aggressive type of fighter, sometimes it is also very effective against a fighter who doesn't expect it. In jeet kune do, this is one of the few times the rear foot is used for kicking from the on-guard position.

Sweep Kick

First, the sweep or reverse kick is seldom used in jeet kune do because, against someone in the same stance as you, the lead hand is always protecting the face. Second, the kick is delivered high and is apt to be caught by an experienced fighter. Third, the kick is not powerful enough to knock your opponent down.

The sweep kick is effective against an unwary opponent who tends to only protect his left side while standing in the right lead position. It is also one of the few kicks that will penetrate against an opponent who habitually leaves his lead foot high above the ground to jam while attacking.

Against someone in the same stance, as in photo 1, Lee begins to deliver a sweep kick, as in photo 2. The delivery of the kick is similar in this case to a front kick and deceives the opponent who attempts a low block. Unencumbered, the kick finds its target, as in photo 3. The path of the kick is from left to right in a semicircular motion, as in photo X and diagram A.

THE PATH OF THE FOOT

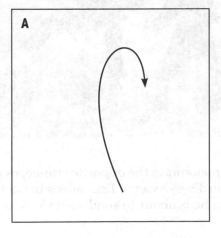

Against an opponent in the opposite stance, as in photos 1 (side view) and 1A (bird's-eye view), Lee moves in such a way that the opponent thinks he is about to send a side kick to his midsection,

as in photos 2 and 2A. While the opponent anticipates the side kick, Lee hits the face by driving his foot above the guarding hand, as in photos 3 and 3A.

Chapter 15
Defense and Counter

Defense and Counter

Counterattacking is a crafty maneuver. First, it is quite safe to use and can be very damaging to your opponent because he is generally caught moving in.

Second, if you are matched against someone equally as skilled as you, you have the advantage because your opponent is bound to expose more of himself as he is leading and committing himself to an attack. In the meantime, you are remaining in the on-guard stance, waiting for the opening. It is preferable to feint your opponent into leading instead of waiting for him to take the initiative.

The art of counterattacking can be applied after provoking your opponent to attack, or by drawing and luring him into attacking by purposely leaving yourself open. The idea of countering is to avoid the blow and hit your opponent while he is off-balance or not in position to guard himself.

Countering requires real proficiency in the art of fighting. It is actually an advanced form of offense. For each lead, there are numerous counters, but you should select the most effective one instantly. This can only be done with constant practice until you are conditioned to react spontaneously.

After countering, follow up by pressing your opponent until he is down, or until he retaliates. Be careful of an opponent who uses the double-hit. His first blow is used to entice you to attack, but his second blow will be the real one, as you attempt to counter it.

Leading Finger Jab

The leading finger jab is a good defensive counterattack weapon for stopping an attack before it unfolds, and as a consequence, it frustrates your opponent. It is easy to employ and is so quick that the opponent gets it in his eye before he can deliver his punch. It is thrown with your fingers outstretched, lengthening the extension of your hand, as in photo A.

It is a good stop-hit weapon, and you should use it at every opportunity during the course of fighting. It enables you not only to score effectively and create openings but can also quickly demoralize an aggressive and confident opponent.

Lee was a skillful exponent of the stop-hit. Here, he shows how to use it against an opponent standing in the opposite stance,

as in photo 1. Lee quickly moves in as he sees the opponent's swing coming, as in photo 2. With his lead hand, which has to travel a much shorter distance than it would with a swing from the rear hand, Lee thrusts the finger jab toward his opponent's face, as in photo 3. Lee constantly keeps his guard hand high to block, as in photo 4.

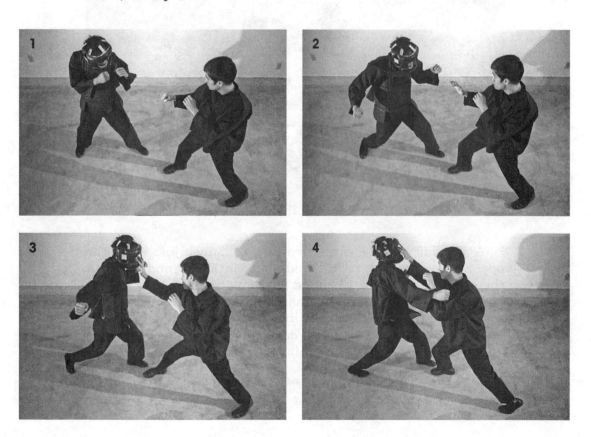

A stop-hit must be correctly timed to launch just when the opponent begins his attack. The idea is to anticipate and intercept the attacker in his path and, at the same time, deliver a blow, keeping yourself secure by either moving out of the attacker's reach or by use of other covering. Success depends on proper anticipation and timing as well as hitting the target perfectly.

An effective maneuver against a swinging opponent is to counter-time (broken rhythm) into his action, or you can stop-kick into an advanced target, like the knee, groin, or an exposed area.

In the previous sequence, against someone in the opposite stance, as in photo A, Lee prepares for the attack. As soon as his opponent is about to deliver a straight lead, Lee quickly intercepts the blow and continues with a right finger jab to the opponent's eye, as in photo B. He keeps his rear hand high to protect against any countering. Timing is so important in an attack in development. After anticipating your opponent's line of attack, you intercept his arm or foot and then counter, just as he is about to deliver.

Leading Right

The leading right, like the leading finger jab, is a good defensive punch against a swing because your blow doesn't have to travel too far, as in photo X. Even when the opponent initiates the punch, you can beat him to his delivery. Besides, against a wild swinger or a slow-moving opponent, you can really frustrate and disturb him with constant blows to his face to keep him

from setting up a defense.

Against an opponent in the opposite stance, as in photo 1, Lee counters with a straight right lead as the opponent attempts a right swing, as in photo 2. Lee stops the attack when his punch makes contact with the face, as in photo 3.

Actually, the stop-hit is used to arrest an attack as it is unfolding. It can be an indirect or direct attack. It may be used while the opponent steps forward to punch or kick, while he is feinting, or while he is moving between a complicated combination.

Against someone standing in the opposite stance, as in photo A, who attempts a swing with his left lead, Lee counters quickly, as in photo B. He counters when he sees the opponent draw his hand to launch his attack.

Often it is necessary to step or lean forward to employ an effective stop-hit—beyond the opponent's focus. Besides, without taking a step, you may not beat him to the punch.

Shin or Knee Kick

The shin or knee low side kick, as in photo X, which is sometimes referred to as the stop-kick, is one of the most formidable defensive tactics in jeet kune do. If done proficiently, you can stop just about any kind of attack, whether a punch or kick. The concept behind this kick is to beat your opponent to the attack. That means you have to stop your opponent while he is in motion, just before he accelerates or just before he attacks. To do that, you must be much quicker than he is. This trait can be developed by training heavily in the science of awareness or the art of anticipation.

As mentioned earlier, Bruce Lee was always a step ahead of his opponent because of his keen, cultivated awareness. He used to practice constantly to increase his sensitivity of his mobile surroundings.

To employ the low side kick against someone standing in the same position, as in photo 1, Lee studies the opponent's face to anticipate his first move. As soon as the opponent begins his attack, as in photo 2, Lee sweeps his lead hand upward to initiate his momentum. Before his opponent can land his blow, Lee retaliates with a low side kick to his knee, as in photo 3.

If the opponent is in the opposite stance, as in photo 1, and is planning to use his rear foot to deliver a front kick, as in photo 2, Lee quickly meets the attack with his lead foot lifted above the floor to intercept the opponent's kicking foot in midair, as in photo 3. You must realize that the stop-kick is not necessarily a countering blow, but sometimes, it is used strictly to stop or block an offensive maneuver.

An opponent who fights from a crouching position is easier to handle because of his limited maneuverability, as in photo A. His low stance and extended feet restrict him from attacking and retreating quickly. In photo B, Lee just moves away from the

right lead punch thrown by his opponent. Lee was able to move away easily from the punch because a low-stance opponent has to telegraph his movement whenever he tries to stand upright to move forward or backward. After avoiding the blow, Lee delivers a crushing shin kick, as in photo C.

Fighting an opponent who stands in the opposite stance, as in photo 1, is not different from someone whose feet are in the same position as yours. It is probably easier to jam his lead leg because it is aligned with your lead foot. In photo 2, when the opponent lunges, Lee meets the attack directly. Even if the opponent has a head start, Lee's quick reaction stops the attack from materializing, as in photo 3.

Against an opponent in close-range, as in photo A, and who stands in the opposite position, Lee evades a left lead punch and simultaneously delivers a kick to the lead knee, as in photo B. This is a fairly safe countering move because the leg has a longer reach than the hand.

Side Stop-Kick

The side stop-kick is almost like the low shin and knee kick, except that the former is employed more devastatingly because the kick is directed at a higher target, as in photos A and B. The side stop-kick is used not only to stop the attack but also to knock the opponent down.

The kick is used extensively because it can be used in medium-distance and far-distance fighting, and it is the most powerful blow available in jeet kune do. When delivered properly, you need just one kick to completely stop an opponent.

Against an opponent standing in the opposite stance at a lengthy distance, as in photo 1, Lee is in a secure position and has more time to prepare for an attack, as in photo 2. After studying the opponent's approach, he moves toward him and unleashes a punishing side kick to his chest, as in photo 3. The impact from the kick not only stops the attack but also drives the opponent backward to the floor, as in photo 4.

Proper timing and distance are important in the application of an effective stop-hit. When the distance is wide, the opponent generally needs some kind of planning in his attack. At this moment, you should launch your attack.

A smart fighter doesn't attack until he initially attains control

of the opponent's timing or hand position. He endeavors to draw
the stop-hit by any method to bring his opponent's hand and leg
within range in order to control it.

Usually, the stop-hit is employed with a straight thrust or

kick, but it may be used during a disengagement, counter-disengagement, or while ducking and slipping.

From a medium distance, Lee quickly stop-hits an opponent who attempts to kick with his rear foot, as in photo 1. Once the attack is launched, Lee, without any hesitation, counters by sliding his rear foot forward and employing a right side kick to the opponent's chest, as in photo 2. The hard blow sends the

opponent reeling backward, as in photo 3.

Against an onrushing assault from a medium distance, as in photo A, Lee moves into his opponent as he sees a right swing coming. With a quick lunge—not too deep, as the opponent is closing in—Lee releases a powerful side kick, as in photo B. The blow stops the attack and drives the opponent backward, as in photo C.

A stop-hit is an excellent defense against an opponent who attacks wildly, without any kind of covering, or against an opponent who stands too near. Sometimes you have to angle your body to find the opening and to control the opponent's hand.

Against an opponent in the opposite stance who moves cautiously from a close distance, as in photo 1, Lee carefully waits for the attack. As soon as his opponent moves in with a straight left, Lee steps away slightly, just enough to avoid the blow, as in photo 2.

Then, Lee quickly shifts his footing and utilizes a right side kick, as in photo 3. The kick must be delivered with his body

erect or moving forward. Otherwise, there is no force behind it.

Another way to score is to use a direct or simple attack when the opponent is within distance and doesn't retreat with his parry. To be certain, hit him when he is stepping forward into range, which is when he is transferring his weight forward or when he indicates "weightiness" (a slight shift in weight).

In another close-range fighting scenario, Lee again waits for the opponent's initial action, as in photo A. As soon as the opponent commits himself, Lee steps back slightly, readying both hands against an unexpected blow, as in photo B. Then, he counters with a side kick as he regains his balance, as in photo C.

Sometimes it is wise to cause your opponent to stop-hit fully in order to prevent him from recovering against a parry or a counterattack. But be aware so he doesn't feint a stop-hit and draw you into a trap.

Hook Kick

The hook kick, as in photo A, is one of the fastest and quickest kicks in jeet kune do and is used mainly as an offensive weapon. It can be launched swiftly without telegraphing the delivery. It is a good offensive and countering kick. It lacks power, when compared to the side kick, but it can be used very effectively. It is targeted at your opponent's vulnerable spots.

Against an onrushing attack, as in photo 1, Lee quickly pivots on his rear foot and switches his weight to it. He avoids the rush by moving away from the path of the attack while still maintaining his balance, as in photo 2. Lee stops the attack with a high hook kick to the face, as in photo 3.

Against a cautious opponent who stands from a medium distance, as in photo 1, Lee fakes a right punch to his face, as in photo 2. As the opponent commits himself with his own straight right punch, Lee parries and, almost in one smooth motion, seizes the opponent's right wrist. Then he quickly releases a hook kick to his opponent's groin, as in photo 3.

This sequence of attack is referred to as an attack on completion. After the opponent has lunged, you parry his blow and divert his primary attack. Then you counter while the opponent's body is extended in a lunge or during his act of recovery—there is no movement of your opponent's foot during this brief phase.

Against someone using a compound preparation whereby he steps forward and employs his hand simultaneously, economical trapping is useful to either immobilize or create a reaction so you can punch or kick.

Spin Kick

The spin kick, as in photo A, is a surprise countering tactic. It is not recommended as an offensive or attacking weapon. It is a difficult kick to master, but once you are adept at using it, it may be your best weapon against a skilled opponent.

The spin kick should be used sparingly and mostly against an aggressive straight-line opponent who constantly rushes at you. It is difficult to employ against a countering and defensive opponent.

Lee and his opponent stand at a far distance, feeling each other out, as in photo 1. Suddenly, his opponent rushes forward as Lee prepares to meet the attack, as in photo 2. Lee, a master of the spin kick, delivers a perfect kick to the opponent's face with ease, as in photo 3.

Standing in the medium distance, Lee faces a cautious opponent, as in photo A. Normally, a spin kick is not the tactic to use here, but Lee applies it effectively, as in photo B. This may work if the opponent is not wary or is a slow-reacting fighter.

Chapter 16
Five Ways of Attack
(by Ted Wong)

Five Ways of Attack

During the later years of his life, Bruce Lee began to teach and make notes on combative techniques that he called the "Five Ways of Attack." The techniques and the nomenclature were heavily influenced by Lee's research into fencing.

Simply put, the five ways of attack are:

A: simple angle attack (SAA)

B: hand-immobilizing attack (HIA)

C: progressive indirect attack (PIA)

D: attack by combination (ABC)

E: attack by drawing (ABD)

Simple Angle Attack

The SAA, sometimes referred to as the simple attack, has its roots in fencing. The SAA is the most difficult way of attack to master, which is why it is rarely used. An example of the SAA is the JKD straight lead punch, as in photos 1 and 2. The SAA is extremely important because you have to master this movement before you can move on to any of the other attacks. The other four ways of attack are dependent on how well you perform the SAA. In jeet kune do, the straight lead is the core technique of the art. All other JKD techniques stem from the straight lead. Because of the degree of difficulty involved in being proficient with the straight lead, there is a tendency to ignore its importance, which then leads to a deficiency and segregation in the ability of the practitioner. Further, if you become proficient in the SAA, then you can score any time you move.

The SAA is any simple attack thrown at an unexpected angle. It is sometimes preceded by a feint, though the feint is not necessarily considered part of the SAA. The point is to strike your opponent using the most direct route while catching him at a moment of vulnerability. The SAA is an attack made up entirely of timing and speed; the attacker simply hits his opponent before he can respond defensively.

All forms of attack, including the SAA, require agile maneuvering because they are often set up by readjusting the distance with your footwork. With the SAA, there is an even

better chance of success if the attack is launched when your opponent is moving his arm away from the line of engagement. This is because he is committed to moving in the opposite direction and must alter his course in order to defend himself, leaving him vulnerable and potentially off-balance, as in photos A to C.

Hand-Immobilizing Attack

The HIA is performed by trapping your opponent's head, hair, hand or leg as you strike through the line of engagement. By trapping or immobilizing a part of your opponent's body, you create a safety zone from which to strike. In other words, the HIA forces an opening, as in photos 1 and 2.

Immobilization attacks can be set up by using any of the other four ways of attack and can be performed in combination or alone. Using an HIA at the moment your opponent intends to deliver a blow requires a keen awareness of your opponent's intention as well as your own execution of speed and skill. See Chapter 7 for more on immobilization techniques.

Progressive Indirect Attack

The PIA is preceded by a feint or an uncommitted thrust, which is designed to throw off your opponent's actions in order to give you time to hit the opening line at the moment of vulnerability. The term "progressive" can be interpreted as "closing distance," and the term "indirect" can be interpreted as "gaining time." The SAA is performed in a single, forward motion without withdrawal, as opposed to the PIA, which is preceded by a feint and consists of two separate movements.

The PIA can be used to simultaneously and effectively bridge the gap and create an opening. The key is for the feint to mask the fact that you are beginning to lunge and, therefore, closing the distance between you and your opponent. In particular, if your opponent's defense is tight, the PIA can be used to force your opponent's hands to move, thereby creating an opening. In order for this to be effective, a feint or false thrust must appear so real that it convinces your opponent to react, as in photos A to C.

Attack by Combination

The ABC is a series of thrusts or strikes that follow each other naturally and are thrown to more than one line. The thrusts are a series of setups designed to maneuver your opponent into a particular position or create an opening so that the final blow in the series will find the vulnerable spot.

Triple blows are common in the ABC. The first two blows are used to bring down your opponent's guard, opening him up for the final strike. Another version of the triple blow is known as the "safety triple." The safety triple is a series of blows, which have as their basis a particular rhythm. In the safety triple, the last blow in the series is aimed in the same location as the first blow; a potential combination would be head-body-head or vice versa, as in photos 1 to 3.

With the ABC, it is important to be able to change your path at any moment to take into account the reaction of your opponent. This is the difference between a novice and an expert. The expert fighter makes use of each opportunity as it presents itself, following up effectively on each opening by creating another until the final clean shot can be delivered.

Attack by Drawing

The ABD is an attack or counterattack that you initiate by luring your opponent into an offensive commitment. This trap causes your opponent to think that he has an apparent opening or to fall into a definitive rhythm and/or pattern that you will then intentionally break. The ABD lures your opponent into a false sense of security and makes him think that he has scored an opening. Your opponent's commitment to a particular course of action will deprive him of the ability to change his course effectively, as in photos A to C.

The difference between the PIA and ABD is intention, whether your goal is to create an opening (PIA) or to create a counter (ABD). The PIA uses a feint to create an opening for a primary attack. The ABD uses a feint to draw a lead, which you would then intercept in a secondary attack. You can use the PIA, or any of the other ways of attack, to set up the ABD. The ABD is more like a chess game; it is calculated to purposefully make an opening that draws your opponent in for your counterattack.

The basic and advanced techniques described in this work can be viewed as the necessary tools you must hone in order to successfully execute the five ways of attack. A thorough review of the techniques is recommended for success.

CHAPTER 19

Chapter 17
Attributes and Tactics

Attributes and Tactics

Speed

A person must have certain attributes to be a skilled fighter. The attributes may be learned or innate. For instance, speed is an innate trait, but it can also be developed further. If you are born without speed then you have to practice daily to acquire it. Or if you do have innate speed and want to increase it, you must train. For more on speed training and specific exercises, see Chapter 5.

There are several different types of speed:

A: Perceptual speed is the quickness and ability of your eyes to see an opening through the action or inaction of your opponent.

B: Mental speed is the ability of your mind to rapidly select the right techniques to attack or counter against an opponent.

C: Performance speed is your ability to accelerate your body, feet or hands from a starting or set position and continue to increase that speed once your body is in motion.

D: Initiation speed relies on correct body position and mental preparedness, so your movements are efficient and direct. Your intention should be direct and waste no movements. Initiation speed is also based on economy of motion.

E: Alteration speed is the ability to change direction quickly in midmotion. It is the capability to alter your direction while in flight.

Speed is a confusing attribute. It comprises several elements, such as your mobility, springiness or resilience, stamina, and physical and mental alertness (the time needed to recognize an attack and react). The more complex the situation, the slower you tend to react because it takes your mind a longer time to figure out what to do.

The following aspects are needed to attain greater speed: (1) warming-up exercises to reduce blood viscosity and increase your flexibility; (2) a suitable stance; (3) visual and audio awareness; and (4) quick-reacting habitual patterns.

Visual awareness or keen perceptual speed must be learned through constant practice because it isn't inherited. It should be part of your daily training—just a short, concentrated practice to perceive rapidly. But this should be supplemented with longer training outside the dojo, as explained in Chapter 5.

When your perception is directed on a simple concept or trigger, such as hearing a gun going off or the dropping of a flag, your perceptual speed will become faster. You can learn to react almost to your full capacity with a simple act with practice. In other words, your improvement of your keen awareness can shorten your reaction time.

The following reasons can lengthen your reaction time: (1) You are exceptionally emotional, (2) tired, (3) not trained, or (4) you lack concentration.

Choice reaction requires more comprehension and deliberation than simple reaction, which is instinctive, quick and very accurate. Like speed, if you have to concentrate on more than one item or action, your reaction will be slower because each one requires some degree of concentration before you can respond.

During training, you should reduce unnecessary choice reactions and, if possible, present your opponent with a variety of probable responses, forcing him into a slower, choice-reaction position.

Your opponent's reaction time is lengthened when the visual-awareness stimuli are combined—such as when an opponent inhales, when he has just completed his technique, when his attention or perception is distracted, and when he is off-balance.

A person who is slow in responding to and delivering attacks can overcome this disadvantage through quick perception. An offensive fighter, who can use only his right foot and right hand extensively, should learn to use both hands and both feet. Displaying a one-sided offense allows your opponent to have the advantage because he knows that your attacks will be limited primarily to one side.

In photos 1 and 2, perceptual speed, initiation speed and performance speed are illustrated. Both the person striking and the person holding the mitt play active roles in practicing their speed training. The person holding the mitt is practicing his perceptual speed (the quickness of his eyes to perceive the motion of his opponent) and his initiation speed (the ability to nontelegraphically strike or counter his opponent simply and directly). The person striking is practicing his performance speed (the ability to bridge the gap, i.e. contract his muscles and move from a set position quickly to cover the distance) as well as his initiation speed.

Timing

Working in concert with speed is the principle of timing. Timing means the ability to recognize the right moment and seize the opportunity for action. This perfect moment may be either seized instinctively or provoked consciously. There are several instances when a hit may be made before, during or after your opponent's actions.

A hit may be made as your opponent is preparing or planning to move, as in photos A and B. Before a movement, you may notice your opponent's concentration flagging, or that he is not paying

close attention. This is an opportune time to strike and catch him off-guard. You should always engage your keen awareness so as to instinctively intercept your opponent's intention or lack of concentration as an opportunity you can exploit to your benefit.

A hit may also land when your opponent is in the middle of a movement, as in photos 1 to 4. During your opponent's attack is the key time to intercept his movement and strike. When your opponent is fully committed to an offensive strike, he is not generally able to counter successfully.

A hit may also land after your opponent's attack is foiled or spent as in photos A to E. The timing here is to attack while your opponent is extended into a lunge or during his act of recovery. During recovery, your opponent is not at his full capacity to defend, so this is an opportune time to strike.

Attitude

An athlete with a winning attitude is self-confident and relaxed. He feels in command of a situation, but he may also experience the physical effects of nervousness ("butterflies in the stomach"), such as nausea or vomiting before the event. This condition is quite natural among novices as well as many experienced athletes.

Once the confident athlete is in the ring or on the field, he is able to control his emotions and perform at his highest peak. But a novice or a champion who is so intent on winning may continue to be so tense that his muscles begin to work against him. He becomes stiff and his motion becomes awkward.

A fighter must not take a lackadaisical attitude toward a fight. He should learn to compete and practice at full speed continuously and not just perform moderately with the idea that he can increase his tempo at any time. A real competitor trains and competes at top capacity—harder and faster than normally required. He develops a good mental attitude.

Experience sometimes shows that an athlete can perform up to this capacity as long as needed. His latent energy ("second wind") does come into play if he performs at his limit.

But the experienced and older athletes do not waste their energy either. A great athlete conserves his energy by using his skills more effectively. He employs fewer wasteful motions through economy of motion.

To improve his performance, momentum should be used at a minimum, especially if it takes great muscular effort. Instead, momentum should be utilized to overcome resistance. You should understand that curved motions demand less effort than straight-line movements, such as when your direction has to change suddenly and sharply.

You must understand that it is a natural tendency to over-mobilize or overexert your effort when confronted with an un-familiar task. You should train with an easy and natural rhythm so your performance will be smooth and automatic. When your initiating muscles are not restricted, your movements will be more accurate and easy.

Becoming a champion requires a good mental attitude toward preparation. You have to accept the most tedious task with pleasure. The better prepared you are to respond to a stimulus, the more satisfaction you will find in the response. The less prepared, the more irritated you will feel when you have to perform.

Tactics

A fighter can be classified either as a mechanical or an intelligent fighter. The mechanical fighter fights in a similar pattern in each encounter. His strikes are repetitious and automatic.

An intelligent fighter will alter his tactics in order to use the right strikes, depending on his opponent's technique and the way he fights. He approaches each encounter with a strategy based on preliminary analysis, preparation and execution.

The preliminary analysis is made during the initial encounter. It consists of studying your opponent's habits, weaknesses and strengths. Is he aggressive or is he defensive? What are his dominant offenses and defenses? You may have to use false attacks to compel him to reveal his speed, reaction and skill.

Preparation comes after understanding your opponent's fighting ability. You now have at least a plan to outwit your opponent, taking advantage of his weakness. If you are planning to take the offensive, you must control the situation. You may mislead him with false attacks, followed by real attacks, by varying your attacks to keep your opponent confused and occupied so he can't assume the initiative. You must be prepared to parry if your opponent attempts a surprise stop-hit or counter.

Although the preparation and attack form one smooth motion, they should really be two separate movements to prepare you against a possible counterattack.

You should be able to halt rapidly and effortlessly when advancing for the preparation needed for an attack. Pay close attention to your balance and foot movement. Short, rapid steps are easier to control than lengthy ones.

Often, especially in close fighting, you can attack on the preparation or arrest of your opponent's motion before he can make his plan materialize. This generally includes some movements to deflect the opponent's lead or cause a reaction for an opening when the feints fail. It also allows a change of distance.

An attack by preparation can also be applied against an opponent who maintains an accurate distance and thereby is difficult to reach because he secures his position by staying constantly out of the attacking range. To reach him, you have to draw him into range by taking a short step back.

If you repeat an attack by preparation too often, it will attract a stop-hit rather than a parry. So initiate it with great economy, eliminating or shortening the time of vulnerability by just opening the lines enough to trap. Practice preparations during engagement, change of engagement, and feints on your partner.

Execution of your real attack demands surprise, quickness, fluidity and good timing. Your thoughts must be decisive, alert and pragmatic. If your opponent seizes the initiative, you may regain it by disturbing his concentration through the constant threat of counterattacking by attacking his outside line, or by beating his guard.

Tactics are the ability to think a step ahead of your opponent. This requires good judgment, the ability to see the openings, a skill in anticipation and "guts." Mechanical ability is a must in order to carry out your strategy. But mechanical perfection alone does not ensure success. You must be able to use your technical ability to intelligently analyze your opponent.

A good fighter first controls his distance with superior footwork and then he continues to lead the opponent's rhythm with feints, false attacks and short but effective hitting.

Learn to use your own rhythm to confuse your opponent, then surprise him with a burst of quickness. Another effective method is to use the broken-time attack, which is a slight pause just before the impact. This will disrupt the opponent's defense.

A novice's rhythm, likewise, may be hard to judge because of its irregularity. A beginner also may not be able to follow your lead. He may panic and parry too soon, in the form of an uncontrolled whip with no direction, and accidentally catch your arm. To avoid this, learn to be patient and only use simple or direct attacks swiftly when there is an opening. Refrain from using compound attacks.

A novice's irregular rhythm may come as a broken-rhythm attack unintentionally and may even fool more skilled fighters who do not expect such a rhythm. In such a case, keep your distance and let your clumsy opponent overreach before countering.

A clever fighter does not fight the same way against all his opponents. He varies his tactics with direct and complex attacks and counters. He also alters his distance and position against each opponent.

One rule is not to use complicated techniques unless they are necessary to achieve your goal. First, use simple movements, and if they don't work, introduce more complex ones. Simple attacks from the on-guard position will often catch your opponent off-guard, especially after a series of false attacks and feints. The defender expects a complex action or a preparation and is not ready for the swift and nontelegraphic blow. To connect against a good fighter with a combination is gratifying and reveals your knowledge of techniques, but to hit him with a simple and direct blow shows great proficiency in your ability.

Half of your fight is won if you know what your opponent is doing. Against a calm, patient fighter who protects himself well in the ready position, who avoids any preparation and who stays out of range, do not attack directly. Such a fighter is normally well-versed in stop-hitting and stop-kicking. Against such a fighter, draw his stop-hit with good feints, then retaliate with trapping or grappling. Your feints should be longer.

But against a nervous fighter, your feint should be shorter. You should agitate a nervous fighter but remain relaxed against both the nervous and calm fighters.

A shorter man has the inclination to attack the advanced targets to overcome his shorter reach. He prefers close fighting if he is stronger. Against such an opponent, fight without moving closer or extending your on-guard position to disturb and restrict his strategy.

A tall fighter is usually slower but has a longer reach that can do damage. Against such a fighter, keep a safe distance until you can close in. Also keep your distance against a fighter who continues to use renewed attacks or keeps on advancing. But do not constantly step back on the attacks, as this is what he wants you to do. Instead, step forward into his attack to unbalance his maneuver.

It is important that you always reverse the tactics used by your opponent. For instance, use counters against an opponent who likes to use stop-hits and use stop-hits against an opponent who uses feints. Box a fighter and fight a boxer. But, ironically, it is not smart to constantly attack a defensive opponent.

Awkward fighters use exaggerated and unexpected movements. Against such a fighter, stand at a distance and parry at the last instant. Because his attacks are simple and direct, your most effective weapon is a stop-hit or a timed hit.

Use a renewed attack with a quick lunge on an opponent who has the tendency to withdraw his hand or foot when a blow is launched toward it. Often, a series of high feints will open the low-line areas, especially around the knee and shin.

During real combat, keep your eyes glued on your opponent. In close fighting, watch his lower line to protect your face, and in long-range fighting, watch his eyes. Keep him on the defensive and keep him guessing. Strike from all angles and press him once you have him in trouble. Draw him to step forward, and when he does, attack him. Concentrate your attacks on his weaknesses and make him fight "your fight," not his.

The difference between an amateur and an expert is that an expert can quickly perceive and seize an opportunity. He makes use of his arsenal and intelligence, delivering punches and kicks in a well thought out manner, creating opening after opening until he delivers a powerful, damaging blow.

PART IV
SELF-DEFENSE TECHNIQUES

Chapter 18
Defense Against a Surprise Attack

The best defense against a surprise attack is not to be surprised. In other words, Bruce Lee always emphasized that a martial artist must constantly be aware of his surroundings. He must train to be cautious and alert at all times. He should never be caught napping before an attack.

In the following segments of self-defense, you will quickly notice that most of the attacks against Lee are prevented because of his alertness.

Lee attempted here to re-enact realistic scenarios that could occur in anyone's daily life. He always believed that the best defense is to be quicker than your assailant.

But to do this, you must practice constantly. All techniques must be done fluidly and with power and swiftness.

Attack From the Side

Walking down the street, Lee notices someone standing at the corner, as in photo 1. Instead of walking near him, Lee leaves enough room to defend against an ambush, as in photo 2. As the assailant attacks, as in photo 3, Lee counters with a quick and powerful side kick to the forward knee, as in photo 4. The kick is followed through completely so it causes the assailant to

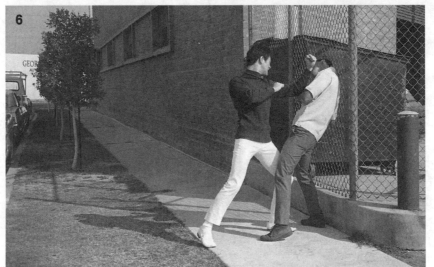

reel backward, as in photos 5. Lee counterattacks with multiple hooks and straight punches to the face, as in photo 6, keeping the assailant off-balance.

Note: You have to constantly practice the side kick on a heavy bag—preferably about 70 pounds—to develop good power. Notice that Lee delivers his kick while keeping his body away from the assailant.

Attack While Entering a Car

As Lee attempts to enter his car, he is aware of the assailant, as in photo 1. As the assailant attempts to kick, Lee surprises him by countering with a side kick to the knee, as in photos 2 and 3. The kick drops the assailant to the ground, as in photos 4 and 5. Lee follows up with a hook kick to the head, as in photo 6.

Note: It seems that the assailant has the advantage over Lee, but anyone who has seen Lee perform knows how fast he was. Lee is able to counter with a kick because his movement is fluid and quick. To be this quick, you have to practice kicking the air or hitting a light bag. Don't kick hard while practicing this because you may hurt your knees. Solid kicks should be done on a heavy bag.

Ambush From the Rear

The assailant follows Lee, as in photos 1 to 3, but Lee is aware of him and pretends he doesn't see him. Before the assailant can throw a punch, Lee counters with a side or back kick to the assailant's knee, knocking him backward, as in photos 4 to 6. Lee follows up by turning to execute a groin kick, as in photos 7 and 8.

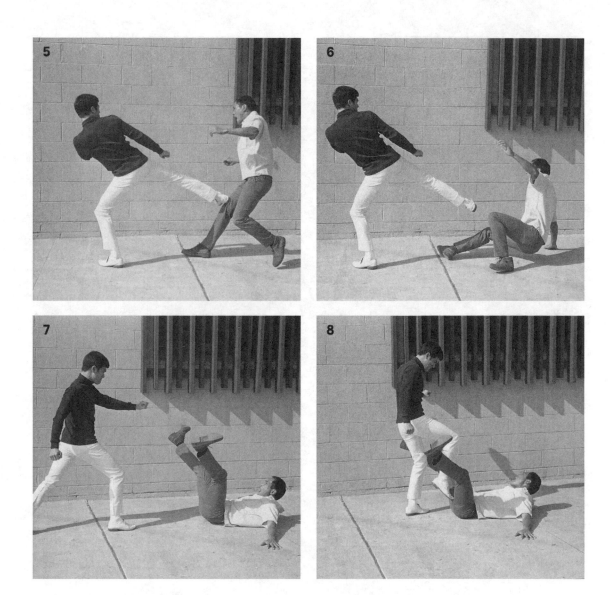

Note: If Lee had turned around to face the assailant, he would have given the assailant the added advantage of preparing for his attack. By being wary and pretending to be unaware, Lee allows himself this added advantage instead.

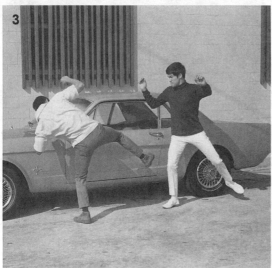

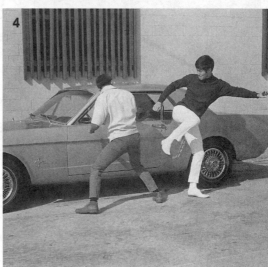

Ambush at Close Quarters

As Lee prepares to enter his car, the assailant rushes toward him and attempts to kick his midsection, as in photos 1 and 2. Lee steps back, as in photo 3. As soon as the assailant places his

foot down, as in photo 4, Lee executes a side kick to the back of the assailant's knee, as in photos 5 and 6. He quickly follows up with a choke hold, as in photos 7 and 8.

Chapter 19
Defense Against
an Unarmed Assailant

Bruce Lee demonstrates how to handle several different forms of assault in this chapter. For years, he kept saying that you are wasting a lot of energy and even making yourself less effective by studying "set patterns" (kata). To him, "fighting is simple and total."

In this chapter, some of the approaches by the attacker may seem irrational. But, as Lee himself said, "There are many irrational people on the streets today."

Defense Against a Crouching Attack

The assailant approaches Lee in a crouch, which is an unusual way of attacking, as in photo 1. From a southpaw stance, Lee delivers a side kick to the side of the forward knee, causing the assailant to drop, as in photos 2 to 4. Lee then follows through by dragging the assailant backward by his shirt collar and finishes him off with a heel stomp to the face, as in photos 5 to 8.

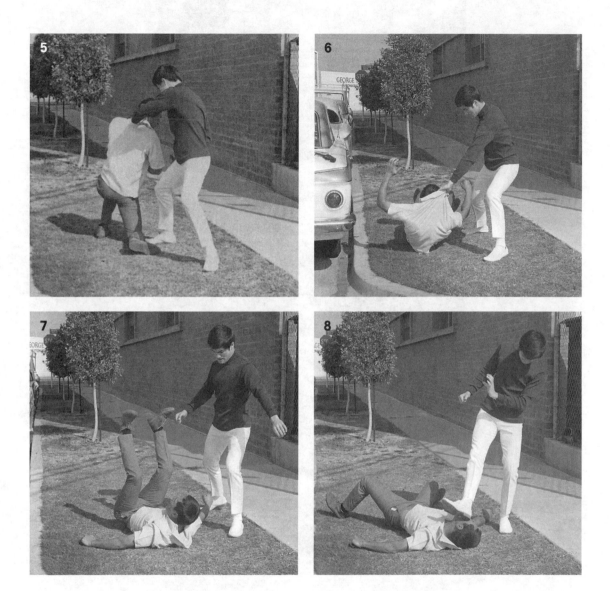

Note: Lee includes this scenario in his self-defense series because some schools of martial arts do not prepare students for situations like this. Besides, some schools teach their students to stop after the opponent is down, but Lee always believed that, because the assailant is trying to maim or kill you, you have to be sure he can't retaliate.

Defense Against a Reverse Punch

In this bird's-eye view, Lee shows how an attack can be nullified by a simple maneuver. As the assailant moves forward to attempt a right punch, as in photos 1 and 2, Lee delivers a side kick to his groin, as in photo 3, with his forward foot.

Note: Many karate schools teach their students to block once or several times before countering. Lee believed that it is more effective to counter immediately, as he has done here. But to do this, you must be quicker than the attacker.

Defense Against a Full Swing

Against a full swing, as in photo A, Lee has more time to counter because the assailant clearly telegraphs his movement. Before the punch can reach him, Lee puts his weight on his rear leg and executes a side kick to the chest, as in photos B and C.

Defense Against a Hook Punch, No. 1

In this view from above, as in photos 1 and 2, we see the assailant attack Lee with an attempted right hook. Lee parries the strike to the side of his head and immediately follows up with a finger jab to the eyes, as in photo 3.

Defense Against a Hook Punch, No. 2

As the assailant attempts a right hook, as in photo A, Lee rotates his hips clockwise, quickly placing his weight evenly on both feet, as in photo B, and executes a finger jab to the eyes without blocking the attack, as in photo C. Lee's striking hand and change of position cause the assailant's punch to miss its mark.

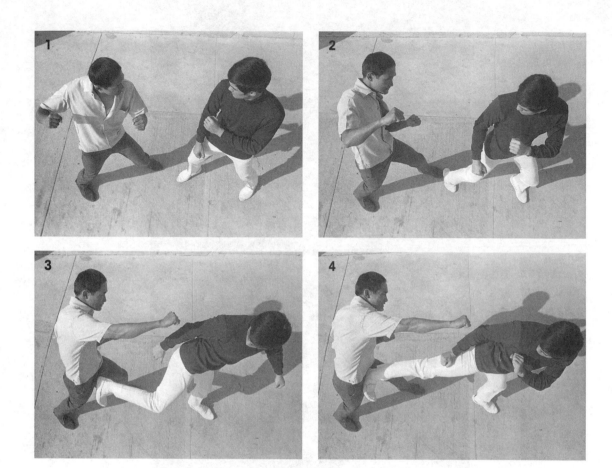

Defense Against a Hook Punch, No. 3

As the assailant attempts a right hook, as in photos 1 and 2, Lee rotates his hip, placing most of his weight on his rear foot. Then he counters with a side kick to the groin, as in photos 3 and 4, using his forward foot.

Note: When defending against a roundhouse punch, Lee has more time to react because the blow is telegraphed, which means he can counter with a side kick by stepping away from the strike before delivering the kick. In the defenses against the hook punch (No. 1 and No. 2), Lee did two variations of the finger-jab counterattack. He personally preferred the second finger jab (see page 381) because of the principle behind economy of movement. (This is the wing chun "inner gate" jab, which can be seen on page 124 of *Wing Chun* by J. Yimm Lee.)

Defense Against a Tackle, No. 1

Like the full-swing attack, Lee has more time to counter against someone who is trying to tackle him, as in photos A to C. As the assailant attempts to tackle him, he steps back and delivers a front kick to his face.

Defense Against a Tackle, No. 2

As the assailant attempts to tackle him, as in photos 1 and 2, Lee just steps back, grabs the assailant's hair and hand, and pulls him to the ground, as in photos 3 to 5. Lee then uses the attacker's own momentum to turn him over, as in photos 6 to 8, so he can stomp on his face, as in photo 9.

Note: Lee always believed that self-defense means that you do anything to get out of a situation or use any way to defend yourself. He normally would not have used the hair tactic in a real fight, but it can be effective in certain situations.

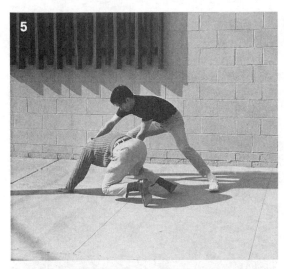

Defense Against a Tackle, No. 3

As the assailant attacks, the defender slides his rear foot back slightly to brace himself, as in photos 1 and 2. The defender grabs the assailant's neck in a head lock as he comes toward him, as

in photos 3 and 4. The defender slides his front foot backward and pins the assailant to the ground while maintaining a choke hold, as in photos 5 and 6. He must execute the pin quickly or the attacker could strike his groin.

Chapter 20
Defense Against Grabbing

When an assailant grabs you, he usually has the jump on you. But it doesn't mean he has the advantage because he doesn't know how you will retaliate.

When you are seized at close quarters, your hands are your most practical defense. You are too close to deliver an effective kick. But a kick can be delivered if the assailant leaves enough distance between you and him. For instance, if he grabs your wrist, you have room to execute a shin or knee kick.

Defense Against a Chest Grab

The assailant seizes Lee's chest with his left hand, as in photo 1, and attempts to knee Lee's groin, as in photo 2. Lee blocks the assailant's knee with his left hand, and in one motion grabs the assailant's left hand while executing a right bottom-fist strike to his groin, as in photos 3 and 4. He then thrusts his left hand into the assailant's throat, as in photo 5, and shoves him backward to the ground, as in photos 6 and 7. Lee jumps, as in photo 8, and executes a well-timed stomp on the assailant's face, as in photo 9.

Note: You have to practice this technique over and over again to do it effectively because there are so many movements involved. In photos 5 to 7, you cannot take your assailant down unless you use one hand to shove his throat while your other hand is used as a lever—grabbing his sleeve and pulling it clockwise and downward.

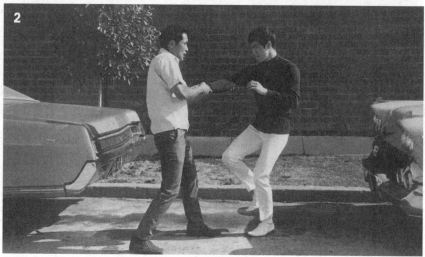

Defense Against an Arm Grab, No. 1

With both hands, the assailant grabs Lee's arm, as in photo 1. Lee quickly faces him, as in photo 2, and delivers an inverted low stomp to the knee, as in photo 3, followed by a punch to the face, as in photo 4. Lee finishes with a left front kick to the groin, as in photo 5.

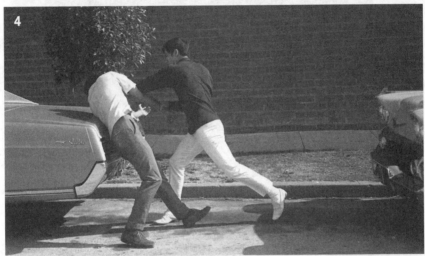

Defense Against an Arm Grab, No. 2

The assailant grabs Lee's arm with both hands, as in photo 1. Without any unnecessary motion, Lee delivers a side kick to the assailant's knee, as in photos 2 and 3.

Defense Against an Arm Grab, No. 3

The assailant grabs Lee's right wrist, as in photo A. Before the assailant can throw his punch, Lee counters with a left cross, as in photo B.

Note: Sometimes a martial arts instructor teaches his students several motions to dispose of an assailant when instead it can be done with just a simple blow, as the above sequence shows.

Defense Against a Belt Hold

The assailant grabs Lee's belt and pulls Lee toward him, as in photo 1. Because he is too close to perform a kicking technique, Lee leans away from the attacker's punch and simultaneously executes a finger jab to the eyes, as in photo 2.

Defense Against a Wrist Lock

The assailant uses a wrist lock on Lee with both hands, as in photo A. Lee quickly turns clockwise, as in photo B, and executes a reverse elbow strike, as in photo C.

Note: Lee always emphasized that you shouldn't turn your back on your opponent, but in this case, it is done quickly enough to be effective without leaving you vulnerable.

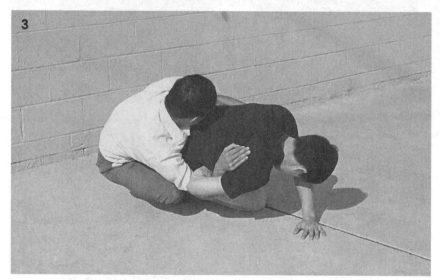

Defense Against a Half Nelson

Attacking Lee from behind, the assailant locks his right arm and keeps his head in a grip, as in photos 1 and 2. Using the attack's momentum, Lee turns his body away from his locked

1

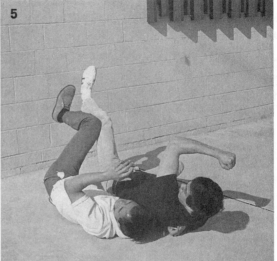

arm (counterclockwise), as in photo 3, forcing the assailant off-balance, as in photo 4. Keeping the assailant's arm locked under his body, as in photo 5, Lee delivers a reverse elbow strike, as in photo 6.

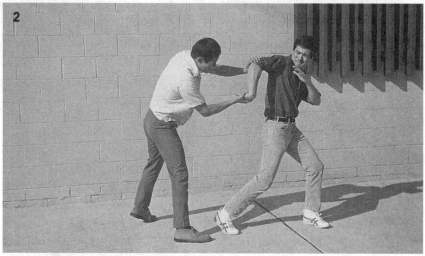

Defense Against a Reverse Wrist Lock

The assailant puts a reverse wrist lock on Lee's right hand, as in photos 1 and 2. Lee retaliates with a side kick to his midsection, as in photo 3, and a spin kick to the same area with the other foot, as in photos 4 and 5.

Note: When someone grabs you with a reverse lock, as in photos 2 and 3, you have to quickly counter before he can pin you to the ground.

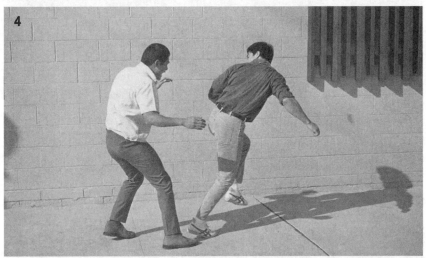

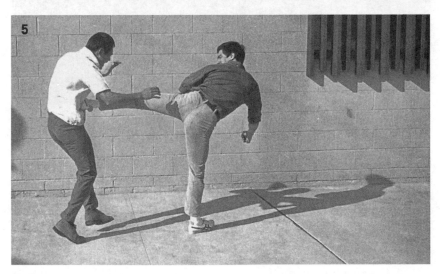

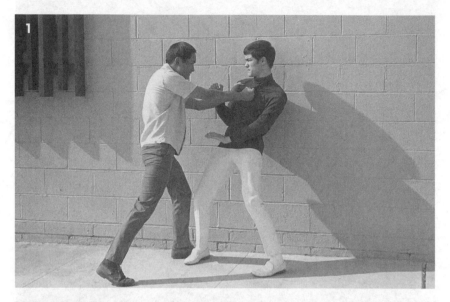

Defense Against a Two-Hand Chest Grab, No. 1

The assailant grabs the front of Lee's shirt with both hands, as in photo 1. Note that Lee uses his left hand to protect his groin. Lee then lifts the same hand to lock his assailant's arm while simultaneously executing a right cross to his face, as in photo 2.

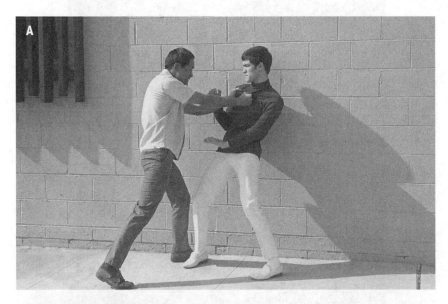

Defense Against a Two-Hand Chest Grab, No. 2

The assailant grabs the front of Lee's shirt with both hands, as in photo A. Note that Lee uses his left hand to protect his groin. Lee then lifts the same hand to lock his assailant's arm. He follows with a forward elbow strike to the helpless assailant's face, as in photo B.

Note: The important maneuver in this technique and the technique before (No. 1) is to trap the assailant's right hand and attack before he can do any damage to you.

Defense Against a Shoulder Grab From the Rear

The assailant grabs Lee's shoulder from the rear, as in photo X. Lee turns his torso and applies a backfist to the assailant's face, as in photos Y and Z.

Note: To have power in your backfist, you have to step back slightly and rotate your hip while simultaneously applying the punch.

Defense Against a One-Hand Chest Grab

The assailant grabs Lee's chest with his left hand and delivers a right swing to Lee's face, as in photos 1 and 1A. Lee doesn't bother to block it but instead applies a straight inner-finger jab to the assailant's eyes, as in photos 2 and 2A. He follows up by immobilizing the assailant's hand and simultaneously hitting him with a right uppercut, as in photos 3 and 3A.

Note: Performing a finger jab simultaneously against a swing looks easy but it isn't. You have to practice this constantly to get it right. This technique comes from wing chun kung fu. (See page 124 of *Wing Chun* by J. Yimm Lee.)

Defense Against a High Reverse Wrist Lock

The assailant applies a high reverse wrist lock to the defender's left hand, as in photos 1 and 2. The defender turns clockwise and executes a back kick, as in photos 3 and 4.

Note: It isn't common for someone to catch you in a reverse wrist lock, but in case it does happen, you should be ready.

Defense Against a Back Arm Lock

The assailant grabs the defender with a rear arm lock that is difficult to get out of, as in photo 1. The quickest way to escape is to execute a back kick to his groin, as in photo 2.

Note: Sometimes a knowledgeable assailant will place his foot and body so close to you that you can't retaliate with a kick. In a case like that, you can always maneuver your body so there's enough space to deliver it.

Defense Against a Chest Grab and a Punch

The assailant grabs the front of the defender's shirt and attempts to punch his face, as in photo A. The defender grabs the assailant's wrist with his left hand and, at the same time, delivers a punch to the assailant's jaw, as in photo B. He follows up with a foot sweep, as in photos C to E.

Note: Instead of a punch to the assailant's jaw, a finger jab will be just as effective. After dropping the assailant, you can then strike him with your hand or foot.

Chapter 21
Defense Against
Choke Holds and Hugs

A good martial artist is always alert and should never be surprised. The following self-defense techniques apply to situations in which you are surprised and must free yourself from a choke hold or a hug.

Bruce Lee always explained that the best defense is the most simple and effective—especially against a choke hold. Lee demonstrates how you can escape and retaliate through direct and simple counters.

In this section, he also demonstrates the use of elbows and strikes that target the groin.

Defense Against a Front Choke, No. 1

The assailant chokes Lee, so he seizes the assailant's wrist to relieve the pressure on his neck, as in photo 1. Maintaining his safety grip with one hand, Lee quickly finger jabs the assailant's eyes, as in photos 2 and 3. He then follows up with a knee strike to the assailant's groin, as in photos 4 and 5.

Note: Lee doesn't waste time in his action here. Instead of trying to break the grip first, he counters directly. Notice that Lee's right foot is touching the assailant's right foot. This is to prevent the assailant from kicking or kneeing him.

Defense Against a Front Choke, No. 2

The assailant chokes Lee and drives him against the wall, as in photo 1. Lee steps out to the side and delivers a front kick to his groin, as in photo 2.

Note: As the assailant chokes him, Lee is able to get out of the choke and move slightly back far enough to do a front kick.

Defense Against a Head Lock, No. 1

The assailant has Lee in a head lock, as in photos A and B. Lee quickly retaliates with a finger jab to the assailant's eyes, using his free hand, as in photo C.

Defense Against a Head Lock, No. 2

The assailant has Lee in a head lock, as in photo 1. Lee is able to place his right hand over the assailant's shoulder and claw at his face, as in photos 2 and 3.

Defense Against a Head Lock, No. 3

The assailant has Lee in a head lock, as in photo A. Lee turns his body in close to the assailant and, with his free hand, as in photo B, pounds at the assailant's groin, as in photo C.

Note: Whenever you are caught in a head lock, you must act fast with a counter or else the assailant will drag you to the ground, making it harder to free yourself.

Defense Against a Rear Stranglehold

The assailant strangles Lee from the rear and also seizes his right hand, as in photo 1. Lee moves slightly to his right and applies a left elbow strike to the assailant's ribs, as in photo 2.

Note: The assailant is trying to strangle Lee and bend his body backward, but before he is put in a vulnerable position, Lee moves to the right and has a clean shot at the assailant's exposed rib area.

Defense Against a Bear Hug (Arms Pinned)

The assailant has Lee in a bear hug, as in photo A. To get out of this, Lee steps his right foot out, drops his weight down slightly to loosen the assailant's grip, and executes a left-hand strike to his groin, as in photo B.

Note: This maneuver requires constant practice because there are several coordinated moves you have to do in a split second. This is especially true if the assailant is a strong person.

Defense Against a Bear Hug (Arms Free)

The assailant has Lee in a bear hug, but his arms are free, as in photo 1. Instead of attempting to free himself from the grip, Lee just delivers a reverse elbow strike to the assailant's face, as in photo 2.

Note: When delivering the blow with your elbow, rotate your hip for added power.

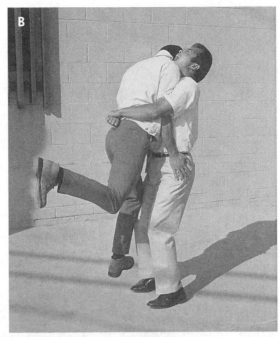

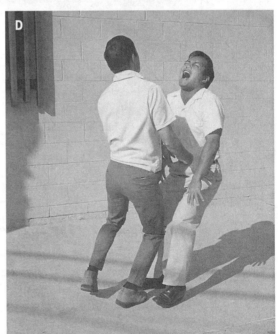

Defense Against a Lifting Front Bear Hug

The assailant grabs the defender from the front and lifts him off his feet, as in photo A. The defender swings his foot back and delivers an upward knee strike to the assailant's groin, as in photos B to D.

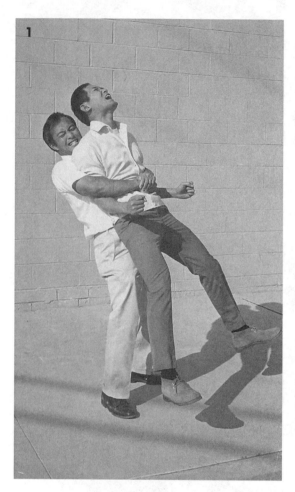

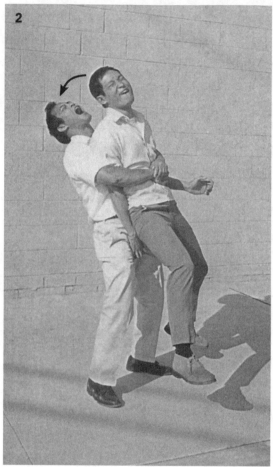

Defense Against a Lifting Rear Bear Hug

The assailant grabs the defender from the rear and lifts him off his feet, as in photo 1. The defender swings his head back and bangs it against the assailant's face, as in photo 2.

Note: To defend against the front bear hug, you have a second or third chance to strike even if you miss the groin because the assailant can't do anything to you as long as he keeps hugging you. For the rear bear hug, you take a risk of getting your head cut open, but the assailant will sustain injuries, as well.

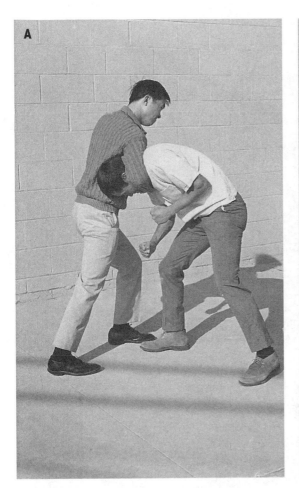

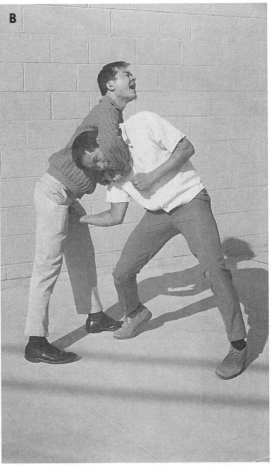

Defense Against a Front Head Lock

The assailant has the defender in a front head lock, as in photo A. Before he can drop him to the ground, the defender takes aim and punches the assailant's groin, as in photo B.

Note: Sometimes in close-quarters fighting, you can end up in a head lock. The most important thing to do is to counter quickly so you are not pinned to the ground.

Chapter 22
Defense Against an Armed Assailant

Defending against an unarmed assailant is quite different from facing someone with a knife or gun. If you practice self-defense against someone using a toy weapon or a facsimile of a weapon, you might perform a technique with proficiency. But if you face a real gun or knife for the first time, you'll probably have chills down your back or even freeze up, especially when you know that one slip-up could mean death.

Only constant practice can give you a feeling of comfort or confidence, but practice does not represent the conditions of the street. Going against a club or staff is not as frightening as going against a real dagger or gun.

The most dangerous weapon, naturally, is the gun. An assailant wielding a club, knife or staff will telegraph his movement, but with a gun, just a little squeeze of the trigger is all you're going to notice.

Bruce Lee demonstrates some techniques against an armed assailant, but he always emphasized, "You are at a disadvantage against someone with a weapon, so keep away from him."

Defense Against a Club, No. 1

The   swings a club at Lee, as in photos 1 and 2. Stepping back just enough to let the club miss him, as in photo 3, Lee retaliates with a side kick to the assailant's body, as in photos 4 and 5.

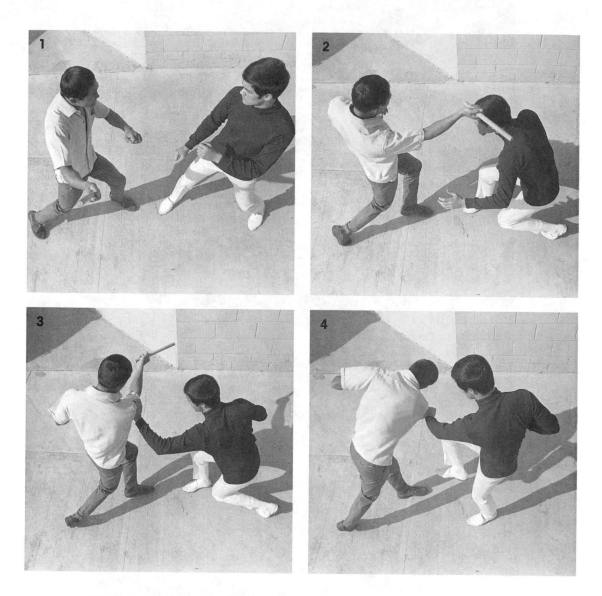

Defense Against a Club, No. 2

The assailant swings his club at Lee, as in photo 1, who ducks under the blow, as in photo 2. Lee then grabs the assailant's sleeve, as in photo 3, forcing him downward. He then immediately counters with a knee to the face, as in photo 4.

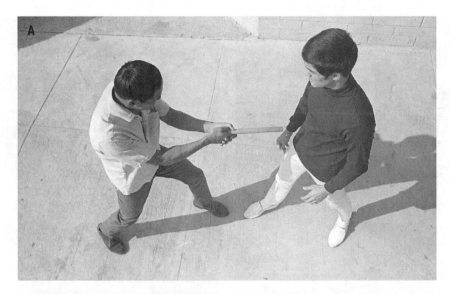

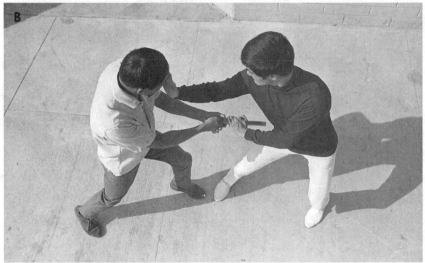

Defense Against a Club, No. 3

The assailant, with both hands on a club, jabs at Lee's midsection, as in photo A. Lee blocks the jab and moves his hips to the side before applying a finger jab to the assailant's eyes, as in photo B.

Note: Against a club or a lead pipe, you must have good timing and know your distance. One slip-up might leave you in grave danger, and you are not given a second chance in most instances. Practice is everything.

Defense Against a Staff: Jamming

In photo 1, the assailant attempts to swing a staff at Lee. Lee moves swiftly toward the assailant, as in photo 2, and jams the assailant's arm with his left hand while punching at the assailant's body with his right, as in photo 3. Holding the as-

sailant's arm, as in photo 4, Lee applies a foot sweep to the ankle
that causes the assailant to fall, as in photo 5. Lee punches him
as he falls, as in photo 6, and finishes him off with a rib stomp,
as in photos 7 and 8.

Defense Against a Staff: Ducking

The assailant swings the staff toward Lee, as in photo 1, and Lee quickly ducks underneath it, as in photos 2 and 3. As soon as the staff passes over his head, Lee quickly counters with a roundhouse kick to assailant's groin, as in photos 4 and 5.

Defense Against a Staff: Eluding, No. 1

In photo 1, the assailant swings a staff at Lee, who moves back just enough to elude the blow, as in photo 2. As soon as the blow passes him, Lee moves in quickly with a high reverse hook kick to the assailant's head, as in photo 3.

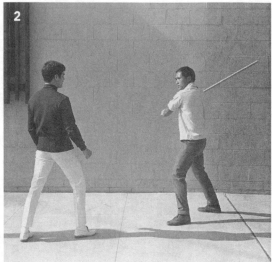

Defense Against a Staff: Eluding, No. 2

In photos 1 to 3, the assailant swings the staff at Lee, who moves back to elude the blow. As soon as the blow passes him,

as in photo 4, Lee jumps in swiftly and applies a reverse hook or
sweep kick to the assailant's face, as in photos 5 and 6.

Defense Against a Staff Thrust, No. 1

The assailant thrusts the staff at Lee's midsection, as in photo 1. Lee sidesteps and seizes the staff, as in photo 2. He follows up with a side kick to the assailant's chest while still holding the staff, as in photo 3.

Defense Against a Staff Thrust, No. 2

In photo A, the assailant thrusts a staff at Lee's midsection. Lee sidesteps and seizes the staff, as in photo B. He then applies a front kick to the assailant's arm, as in photo C.

Note: Against a staff or bo, you have two advantages: The assailant cannot hide his weapon, and he telegraphs his movement more so than with a club or knife. The disadvantage is that he has a longer reach and can hit you from farther away. It is very important that you do not misjudge in closing the distance. Timing is also important in defending against a staff.

Defense Against a Knife: Grab and Stab

The assailant grabs Lee's shirt, as in photo 1, and attempts to stab him with a knife, as in photo 2. Lee quickly seizes the assailant's left hand and swings his right arm into the assailant's

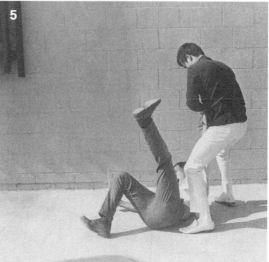

elbow, as in photo 3. In photo 4, Lee also simultaneously trips him with a right foot sweep. As soon as the assailant falls to the ground, as in photo 5, Lee follows up with a crushing foot thrust to the assailant's body, as in photo 6.

Defense Against a Knife Thrust, No. 1

In photo 1, Lee faces an assailant with a knife. Before he attacks, Lee fakes a finger jab to the assailant's face, which causes him to react, as in photo 2. At that instant, Lee kicks him in the ankle, leaving enough space between the assailant and himself to apply the kick, as in photo 3.

Defense Against a Knife Thrust, No. 2

The assailant approaches Lee with a knife, as in photo A. Lee applies a crescent kick to the assailant's wrist, as in photo B, causing him to drop the knife, as in photo C.

Defense Against a Knife Swing

The defender is face to face with an assailant wielding a knife, as in photo 1. When the assailant swings the knife at him, the defender quickly evades the assault by stepping back, as in photo 2. The instant the defender sees an opening after the knife passes by him, as in photo 3, he moves forward and applies a

side kick to the back of the assailant's knee, forcing him to the ground, as in photo 4.

Note: Facing a person with a knife is quite frightening unless you have mentally prepared for this type of situation. If you haven't, you should start right away. If you meet someone with a knife someday, you don't want to freeze up during that moment.

Caution: Always avoid an encounter with an armed person if you possibly can.

Defense Against a Gun: Front

The assailant holds a gun on Lee, as in photo 1. In photo 2, Lee reacts quickly by stepping forward, twisting his hip and simultaneously parrying and seizing the assailant's wrist so Lee

is not in the line of fire. With his free hand, Lee attacks the assailant's throat, as in photo 3, and then he slides his hand down along the assailant's arm until he seizes the assailant's wrist and follows it up with a left backfist, as in photo 4.

Defense Against a Gun: Rear

The assailant points a gun at Lee's back, as in photo 1. Lee retaliates by turning his body counterclockwise and using his arm to parry the assailant's hand and move himself out of the line of fire, as in photo 2. In photo 3, Lee seizes the assailant's wrist and attacks the assailant's throat with his free hand. He follows up with multiple blows to the head, as in photo 4.

Note: As mentioned before, taking a gun away from a person is very risky. There's no way to take away a gun from an attacker from a distance. Before you could even reach the assailant, he only has to squeeze the trigger. The only chance you'll ever have against a gun is at close quarters. Even then, it's difficult, and you can't make any mistakes because there will be no second chance.

Chapter 23
Defense Against Multiple Assailants

If attacked by two or more assailants, then you may be at a real disadvantage unless you are better prepared for fighting than they are. Although Bruce Lee explained that he uses the unorthodox (southpaw) stance while fighting so he can depend mostly on his right foot and hand, you must be able to use both your left and right limbs proficiently against multiple assailants.

Naturally, defending against multiple assailants is harder than against an individual because you have to be cognizant of all your assailants' positions. If you are pinned by two or more individuals, the odds of freeing yourself are heavily against you. Their combined strength and weight might be twice as much as yours.

Defense Against a Rear and Front Attack

Assailant A pins Lee's left hand behind his back and holds his shirt from the rear, as in photo 1. Assailant B throws a right punch to Lee's face, as in photo 2. In photo 3, Lee ducks the blow,

whirls toward his right—freeing his arm from assailant A—and applies a backfist to A's ribs. He then finger jabs assailant B's throat, as in photo 4, and finishes off assailant A with a high side kick, as in photos 5 and 6.

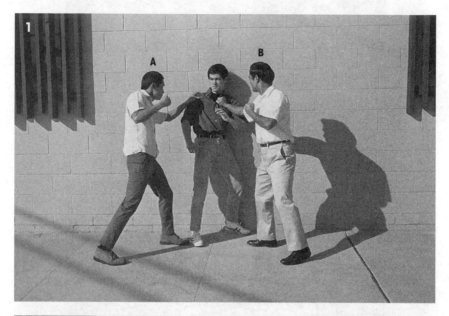

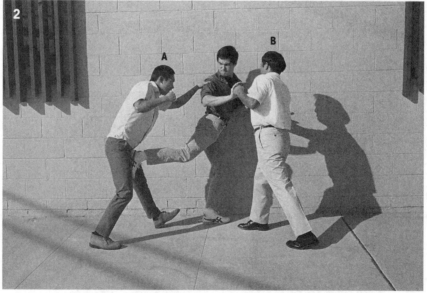

Defense Against Assailants After Being Pinned to the Wall

In photo 1, Lee is pinned to the wall by two assailants. He quickly delivers a side kick to assailant A's groin and blocks the

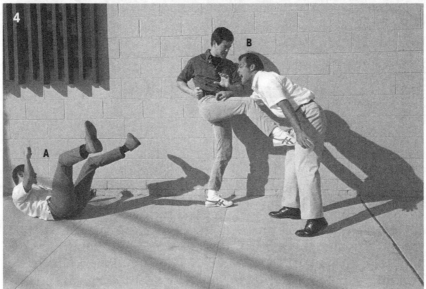

straight left that is thrown by assailant B, as in photo 2. He
follows up with a right cross and a front kick to the groin of
assailant B, as in photos 3 and 4.

Defense Against Assailants From a Lying Position

While lying on the ground, Lee is attacked by assailants from both directions, as in photo 1. In photo 2, Lee uses his hands to stop the kick thrown by assailant A, and he simultaneously applies a thrust kick to assailant B's knee, toppling him to the ground, as in photo 3. Hanging on to assailant A's foot, Lee then applies a forward kick to his groin, as in photos 4 and 5.

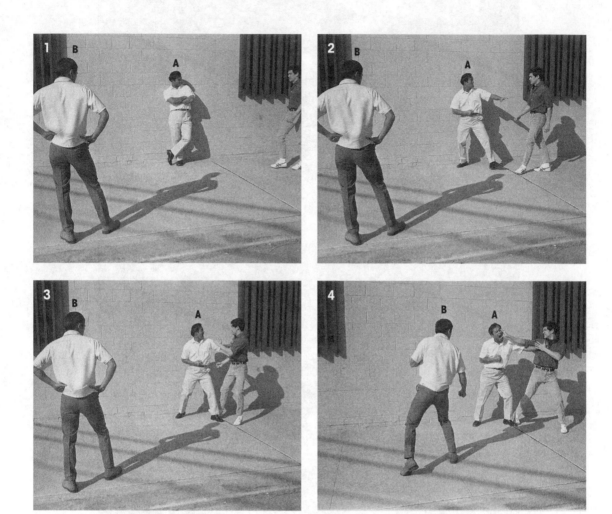

Defense Against an Ambush

As he strolls along, Lee is stopped by assailant A, as in photos 1 and 2. Lee grabs assailant A's wrist, finger jabs his eyes, follows up with a hook to his chin, as in photos 3 and 4, and sends the

assailant tumbling to the ground in front of him, as in photo 5.
When assailant B comes to the aid of his fallen comrade, Lee
greets him with a hook kick to his chest, as in photos 6 and 7.

Defense Against a Bear Hug and a Frontal Attack

Assailant A bear-hugs Lee by pinning his arms while assailant B prepares to swing at him, as in photo 1. In photo 2, Lee counters with a left front kick to assailant B's groin. Lee then

places his left foot back, holds assailant A's arms and flips him
to the ground with a twist of his body, as in photos 3 and 4. Lee
finishes off assailant A with a straight punch to his face, as in
photos 5 and 6.

Defense Against a Bear Hug and Two Frontal Attacks

In photo 1, Lee is pinned in a bear hug by assailant A while assailants B and C prepare to move in. Lee quickly attacks the groin of assailant A, as in photo 2. In photos 3 and 4, with one sweeping motion, Lee throat-chops assailant A with his left hand and punches assailant B with his right. He finishes off assailant C with a side kick to his chest, as in photo 5.

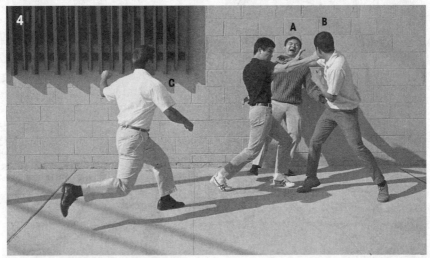

Defense Against a Full Nelson and a Frontal Attack

While held in a full nelson by assailant A, assailant B moves toward the defender, as in photo 1. Leaping high in the air, the defender kicks assailant B's chest, which causes him to reel backward, as in photo 2. As the defender lands on his feet, as in photo

3, he bends forward and raises his right foot, slamming it hard into assailant A's instep, as in photos 4 and 5. As assailant A loosens his grip, the defender counters with an elbow to his face, as in photos 6 and 7.

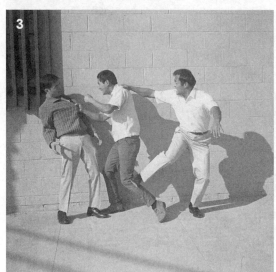

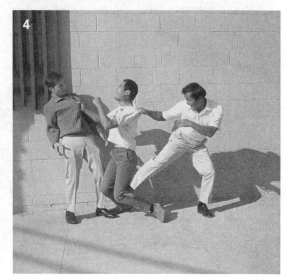

Aiding a Victim or Friend

In photo 1, the defender's friend is being shoved around by a bully. The bully has not seen the defender, so he quickly sneaks up on the bully, as in photo 2, grabs his shoulder, as in photo 3, and delivers a side kick behind his knee, bringing him to his knees, as in photos 4 and 5. Then the defender and his friend grab the bully's wrists, as in photo 6, and pin him to the ground with his face down, as in photos 7 and 8.

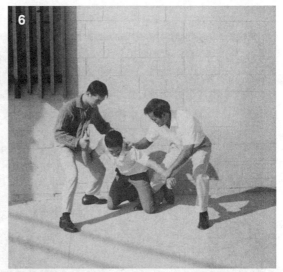

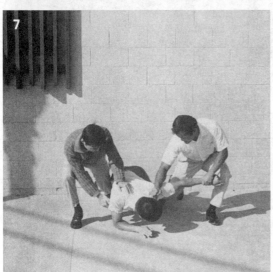

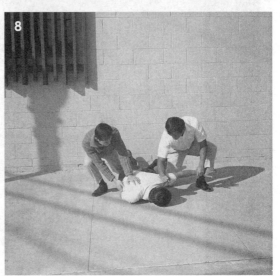

Note: When two or three individuals attack you, they normally are overconfident and attack recklessly. This is an added advantage for you because they are bound to leave an opening that they normally wouldn't leave during a one-on-one encounter. Because you do not usually have a second chance in a multiple-assailant attack, you have to be sure that your techniques are executed with effectiveness. You can't worry about trying not to maim your assailants. You have to give the fight all you've got.

Chapter 24
Defense From a Vulnerable Position

Bruce Lee included this chapter because he believed that an attack can come from anywhere, even while you're sitting in a chair or lying down. Or you could be surprised and have to fight your way from a prone position like when you are pinned on your back.

To Lee, any defense is all right, meaning that your delivery of kicks or punches doesn't have to be beautiful or picturesque. In self-defense, everything goes—any way to get out of a predicament without damaging yourself—whether a scratch, bite, pinch, etc.

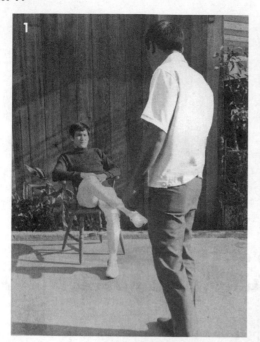

Defense From a Chair: Frontal Attack, No. 1

Sitting in a chair, Lee is approached by an assailant, as in photo 1. Without warning, the assailant rushes him, as in photo 2, and Lee instinctively delivers a front thrust kick to the groin without getting up, as in photo 3.

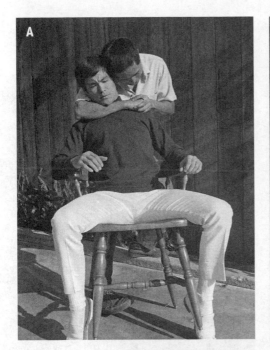

Defense From a Chair: Rear Attack

Lee sits in a chair and is surprised by an assailant who sneaks up from behind him and applies a head lock, as in photo A. In photos B and C, Lee grabs the assailant's hair and applies a finger jab to his eyes.

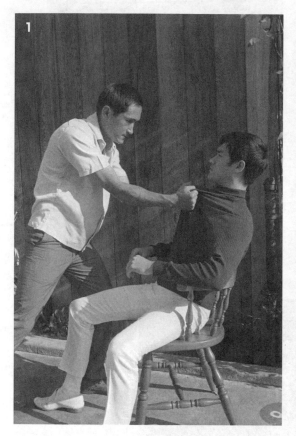 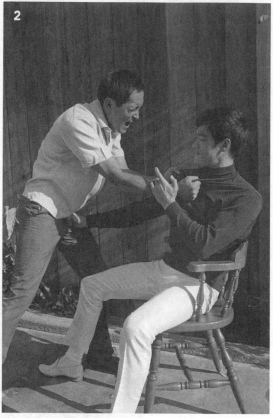

Defense From a Chair: Frontal Attack, No. 2

While sitting in a chair, Lee is surprised by an assailant, who grabs the front of his shirt with both hands, as in photo 1. Lee quickly counters with a right punch to the assailant's groin, as in photo 2.

Note: To apply techniques in any of these attacks, you have to be quick and effective. You are in a disadvantageous position, and a slow reaction on your part might mean further problems. For instance, if the attacker is able to knock you down from the chair and pin you, you have to apply other techniques that are not as simple, and it might take longer for you to free yourself or incapacitate the assailant.

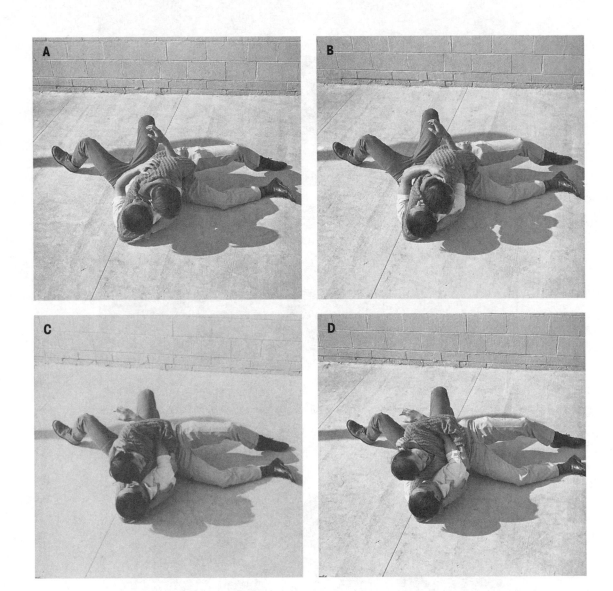

Defense From a Lying Position: Head Lock

In photo A, the defender is pinned by an assailant, who has him in a head lock and has his right hand pinned. Using his free left hand, the defender grabs the assailant's ear and pulls on it until he releases his grip, as in photos B to D.

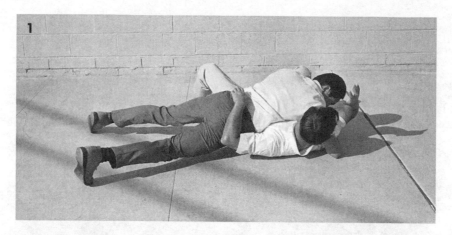

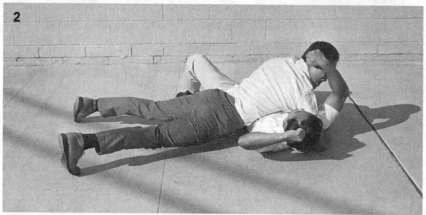

Defense From a Lying Position: Cross-Body

In photo 1, the assailant pins the defender in a cross-body position, leaving his arms free. The defender grabs the assailant's ear with his right hand, as in photo 2, and applies an elbow to his body, as in photo 3.

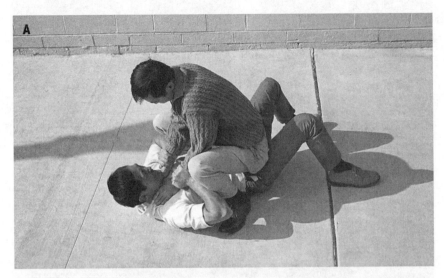

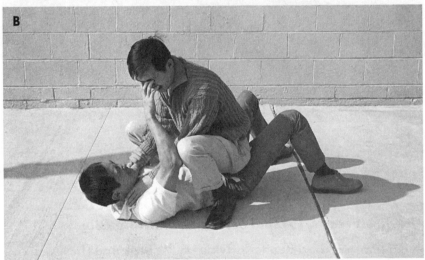

Defense From a Lying Position: Choke Hold

In photo A, the defender is lying flat on his back with the assailant straddling his chest and choking him. The defender grasps one of the assailant's wrists to relieve the choke's pressure, and with the other hand, applies a finger jab to his eyes, as in photo B.

Note: Defending yourself in a prone position is more difficult than in an upright position. First, you are not as mobile. Second, you are limited in your use of defensive techniques like kicking or punching. Third, because of your limited mobility, you can easily be overcome by two or more attackers.

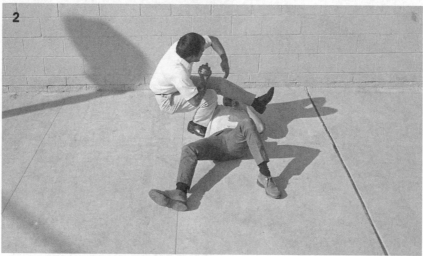

Defense From a Prone Position: Stomping Blow

In photo 1, the defender is lying on his back and the assailant, who is holding the defender's right wrist with both hands, attempts to stomp on his chest. The defender rolls quickly toward the assailant and trips him to the ground, as in photos 2 and 3. Then, he applies a left corkscrew hook to his groin, as in photos 4 and 5.

INDEX

A

Abdominal muscles, 17-19, 27, 76

Aerobic exercises, 8-11

Air bag, 85, 171, 173

Alteration speed, 352

Ambush, 370-373, 458-459

Antagonistic tension, 12, 26

Apparatus and equipment

    air bag, 85, 171, 173

    canvas (wall) bag, 66, 82, 99

    dummy, 76-77, 82, 90, 92, 100, 111, 113-114, 124, 197, 204

    Exercycle, 8

    flexibility, 12-17

    heavy punching bag, 63, 75, 80-82, 99, 111, 114, 163, 168-169, 176-177, 181

    medicine ball, 18

    paper target, 62, 91-92, 103, 110

    punching pad, 64, 82, 97-98, 103, 111, 114, 117

    rubber ball, 76

    shield, 64-65, 83, 85, 171-173

    skipping rope, 8, 10, 48

    speed bag, 95-96

    staff (use of), 55-56, 69, 173, 430-439

    steel cylinder, 68

    weight training, 76

Arm grab, 392-395

Attack by combination, 346

Attack by drawing, 348

Attack entering a car, 368-369

Attack from side, 366-367

Attack, rear and frontal, 452-453

Attack, simple, 238

Attacks with kicks, 287-311

Awareness, 116-117, 320, 353

Axis to generate power, 61

B

Back arm lock, 408

Backfist punch, 88-89, 103, 151, 156, 158, 194, 272-278

Backward burst, 53

Backward shuffle, 44-46

Bad habits in sparring, 162-163

Balance, 32-39

Bear hug, 419-422, 460-463

Beating, 277

Belt hold, 396

Bobbing, 228-231, 247

Boxer, 166

Boxing, 121

Bridging the distance (gap), 289

Broken rhythm, 135

C

Canvas (wall) bag, 66, 82, 99

Cardiovascular system, 8

Center of gravity, 35, 39

Centerline, 146, 156-168, 258

Chair (defense from), 470-472

Chest grab, 390, 402-403, 405, 409

Chi, 69

Chi sao (sticky-hands exercise), 38-39, 70, 72, 74-75, 148, 154-166

Choke, 412-414

Clapping game, 103

Classical style, 42, 50, 95, 97, 139-142, 151, 184, 189, 192, 197-201

Clenching fists, 61

Climbing stairs, 19

Close or infighting, 23, 56, 64, 101, 121-124, 127, 143, 230, 284, 331, 360

Club, 426-429

Compound attack, 239

Counterattacking, 313-337
Counter-disengagement, 328
Counter-time, 316
Crossing feet, 48
Crouching attack, 376-377
Cut-off, 168

D

Decoy or false attack, 263
Defense against an armed assailant, 425-449
  club, 426-429
  gun, 446-449
  knife, 440-445
  staff, 430-439
Defense against an unarmed assailant, 375-387
  crouching attack, 376-377
  full swing, 379
  hook punch, 380-382
  reverse punch, 378
  tackle, 383-387
Defense against choke holds and hugs, 411-423
  bear hug, 419-422
  front choke, 412-414
  front head lock, 423
  head lock, 415-417
  rear stranglehold, 418
Defense against grabbing, 389-409
  arm grab, 392-395
  back arm lock, 408
  belt hold, 396
  chest grab, 390
  chest grab and punch, 409
  half nelson, 398-399
  high reverse wristlock, 406-407
  one-hand chest grab, 405
  reverse wristlock, 400
  shoulder grab from rear, 404
  two-hand chest grab, 402-403
  wrist lock, 397

Defense against multiple assailants, 451-467
  ambush, 458-459
  bear hug and frontal attack, 460-463
  full nelson and frontal attack, 464-465
  lying position, 456
  pinned to the wall, 454-455
  rear and frontal attack, 452-453
Defense against surprise attack, 365-373
  ambush at close quarters, 372-373
  ambush from rear, 370-371
  attack entering a car, 368-369
  attack from side, 366-367
Defense from a vulnerable position, 469-477
  chair, 470-472
  lying position, 473-476
Defensive fighter, 127
Deflecting, 277
Disengagement, 254, 278, 328
Distance, 121-125, 173, 239
  close, 23, 56, 64, 101, 121-125, 127, 142
  far, 130-131, 326
  medium, 122, 128, 284, 291, 297, 326, 329, 333
Double-lead, 152
Drawing, 225
Drop shift, 56
Ducking, 131-132, 328
Dummy, 76-77, 82, 90, 92, 100, 111, 113-114, 124, 197, 204

E

Economy of motion, 359
Equipment (see apparatus)
Endurance exercises, 10-11
Engaging, 272, 361
Evasive tactics, 230
Exercises
  aerobic, 8-11
  cardiovascular, 8

chi sao (sticky-hands exercise), 38-39, 70, 72, 74-75, 148, 154-156

climbing stairs, 19

endurance, 10-11

flexibility, 12-17

forearm, 77

isometric, 74

jogging, 8, 53, 91

leg raise, 14

leg splits, 14, 16

limbering, 17

reverse curl, 77

reverse extension, 77

running, 8

shadowboxing, 10-11, 48

sit-ups, 17

skipping rope, 8, 10, 48

trampoline, 16

warming-up, 12, 353

weight-training, 76

Exercycle, 8

F

False attack, 263

Faulty sparring stances, 222-223

Faulty stances, 27-31

Feinting, 224-225, 242, 299

First line of attack, 166, 211

Fist-and-elbow combination, 96

Five ways of attack, 339-349

simple angle attack, 340-342

hand-immobilizing attack, 343

progressive Indirect Attack, 344

attack by combination, 346

attack by drawing, 348

Flexibility exercises, 12-17, 173

Flicky kick, 79

Flowing energy, 69, 74, 79, 94, 154-161

Footwork, 42-57, 107, 120, 126-135, 204, 214, 230-231

Forearm exercises, 77

Forward burst (lunge), 49-53, 80, 109, 171

Forward drop, 56

Forward (advance) shuffle, 42-46, 103, 174

Front kick, 85, 113-114, 131, 181, 195, 203-204, 320

Full nelson and frontal attack, 464-465

Full swing (defense against), 379

G

Good form, 26, 36

Gun (defense against), 446-449

H

Half-beat, 226

Half nelson (defense against), 398-399

Hand-immobilizing attack, 343

Hand techniques for offense, 237-285

Head lock (defense against), 415-417, 423

Heavy punching bag, 63, 75, 80-82, 99, 111, 114, 163, 168-169, 176-177, 181

High hook kick, 127-128, 134, 172, 174

High side kick, 14

Hips (rotation of), 62-63, 74, 105, 222

Hook kick, 105-112, 174, 233, 297-300, 332-335

Hook punch (defense against), 380-382

I

Initiation speed, 352

Inner gate, 158

Inside high parry, 184-188

Inside kick, 181

Inside low parry, 188-191, 197, 204

Intelligent fighter, 360

Isometric exercise, 74

J

JKD stance, 22, 39, 75-76

JKD delivery of punch, 66-67

JKD movement, 49

Jogging, 8, 53, 91

K

Ki, 69

Kicks

    flicky, 79

    front, 85, 113-114, 131, 181, 195, 203-204, 320

    high hook, 127-128, 134, 172, 174

    high side, 14

    hook, 105-112, 174, 233, 297-300, 322-335,

    inside kick, 181

    polelike, 79

    shin or knee, 288-291, 320-325

    side, 50, 53, 79-85, 105, 112, 128, 134, 166-173, 217, 291-297, 320

    snap, 79

    spin, 176-179, 302-307, 335-337

    stop-kick, 168, 322, 326-332, 362

    sweep, 179-181, 308-311

    thrust, 79

Kinesthetic perception, 37

Knife (defense against), 440-445

Knuckles (toughening of), 66-67

L

Lead jab, 100-101, 146, 272

Lead to body, 250-255

Leading finger jab, 90, 93-94, 103, 151, 156-158, 162, 209-210, 240-244, 314-317

Leading straight left, 256-263

Leading straight punch, 93-96, 100, 103, 138-146

Leading straight right, 245-250, 317-319

Leather strip, 92

Leg raise, 14

Leg splits, 14, 16

Light as feather, 48

Limbering exercises, 17

Long-range sparring, 233

Long-short-short rhythm, 224

Lop sao (grabbing hand), 75-76, 88-89, 154, 156, 191

Low-line, 24, 77, 112, 181, 197, 204, 254, 363

M

Maneuvering, 126

Martial (meaning of), 208

Mechanical fighter, 360

Medicine ball, 18

Mental speed, 352

Mobility, 22, 42

Moving-back maneuver, 128

N

Nontelegraphic, 89, 101-103, 227

O

One-inch punch, 72, 74

On-guard position, 22-39

Oriental martial arts tournaments, 220

Orthodox fighter, 56

Outside high parry, 191-197

Outside low parry, 197, 201

P

Pak sao, 75

Paper target, 62, 91-92, 103, 110

Parrying, 183-205, 238, 333

Perceptual speed, 352

Peripheral vision, 116

Phon-sao (trapping hand), 154

Pinned to the wall (defense against), 454-455

Polelike kick, 79

Power kicking, 77-85

Power training, 60-85

Preparation of attack, 360

Primary attack, 334

Primary targets, 208-211

Progressive indirect attack, 344

Pulling power, 75-77

Punches and jabs

    backfist, 88-89, 102, 151, 156, 158, 194, 270-276

    hook, 380-382

    lead jab, 100-101, 146, 272

    leading finger jab, 90, 93-94, 103, 151, 156-158, 162, 209-210, 239-244, 314-317

    leading straight left, 256-263

    leading straight punch, 93-96, 100, 103, 138-146

    leading straight right, 245-250, 317-319

    one-inch punch, 72, 74

    push-punch, 152

    uppercut, 284-285

    vertical-fist, 72

Punching pad, 65, 82, 97-98, 103, 111, 114, 117

Punching power, 61-75

Push-punch, 152

Q

Quick advance (lunge), 46-47, 49, 170, 174, 329

Quick retreat, 47-48

R

Reaction time, 353

Renewed attack, 258, 363

Reverse curl, 77

Reverse extension, 77

Reverse punch (defense against), 378

Roll-and-trap maneuver, 158

Rolling, 230

Rubber ball, 77

Running, 8

S

Science of fighting, 214, 220

Shadowboxing, 10-11, 48

Shield, 64-65, 83, 85, 171-173

Shin or knee kick, 288-291, 320-325

Short-long-short rhythm, 225

Short-range sparring, 233

Shorten the gap (distance), 122

Shoulder grab (defense against), 404

Shuffle, 42-46

Side stepping, 53-57, 129-135, 284

Simple angle attack, 340-342

Sit-ups, 17

Skill in movement, 119-135

Skipping rope, 8, 10, 48

Slapping match, 101

Slipping, 328

Snap kick, 79

Southpaw stance (see also unorthodox stance), 22-24, 54, 56

Sparring, 220-222

Speed, 226-227, 243

Speed bag, 95-96

Speed in kicking, 105-117

Speed in punching, 88-101

Speed training, 88-117

Spin kick, 176-179, 302-307, 335-337

Staff (defense against), 430-439

Staff (use of), 55-56, 69, 173, 430-439

Steel cylinder, 68

Step-in and step-out maneuvers, 231

Stop-hit, 314-319, 332, 361, 362, 363

Stop-kick, 168, 322, 326-332, 362

Stranglehold (rear, defense against), 418

Sweeping hand, 50

Sweep (reverse) hook kick, 179-181, 308-311

T

Tackle (defense against), 383-387

Tactics, 360-363

Targets, 207-217

Thrust kick, 79

Timed hit, 278, 363

Timing, 225-226, 243-244, 316, 355-359

Trampoline exercises, 16

Trapping or immobilizing, 276-278

U

Unorthodox stance (see also southpaw stance), 22, 132

Uppercut, 284-285

Upper line, 105, 174, 189, 213

V

Vertical-fist punch, 72

Vulnerable spots, 217

W

Warming-up exercises, 12, 353

Weaving, 228-233, 246

Weight-training, 76

Wing chun, 75, 154, 158

Winning attitude, 359

Wrist lock, 397

Wrist lock (reverse), 400, 406-407

TAO OF JEET KUNE DO
by Bruce Lee

This is Bruce Lee's treatise on his martial art, *jeet kune do*.
This international best-seller includes the philosophy of jeet kune do,
mental and physical training, martial qualities, attack and strategy.
208 pgs.
Size: 8-1/2" x 11"
ISBN-13: 978-0-89750-048-7
Book Code 401—Retail $16.95

www.blackbeltmag.com

www.bruceleefoundation.org